GW01019058

DON'T SETTLE
HOW TO
MARRY
THE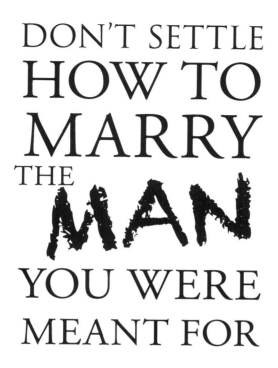
MAN
YOU WERE
MEANT FOR

Scott Carroll, MD

BALBOA.
PRESS

A DIVISION OF HAY HOUSE

Copyright © 2016 Scott Carroll, MD.

All rights reserved. No part of this book may be used or reproduced by any means, graphic, electronic, or mechanical, including photocopying, recording, taping or by any information storage retrieval system without the written permission of the author except in the case of brief quotations embodied in critical articles and reviews.

Balboa Press books may be ordered through booksellers or by contacting:

Balboa Press
A Division of Hay House
1663 Liberty Drive
Bloomington, IN 47403
www.balboapress.com
1 (877) 407-4847

Because of the dynamic nature of the Internet, any web addresses or links contained in this book may have changed since publication and may no longer be valid. The views expressed in this work are solely those of the author and do not necessarily reflect the views of the publisher, and the publisher hereby disclaims any responsibility for them.

The author of this book does not dispense medical advice or prescribe the use of any technique as a form of treatment for physical, emotional, or medical problems without the advice of a physician, either directly or indirectly. The intent of the author is only to offer information of a general nature to help you in your quest for emotional and spiritual well-being. In the event you use any of the information in this book for yourself, which is your constitutional right, the author and the publisher assume no responsibility for your actions.

Any people depicted in stock imagery provided by Thinkstock are models, and such images are being used for illustrative purposes only. Certain stock imagery © Thinkstock.

Print information available on the last page.

ISBN: 978-1-5043-6810-0 (sc)
ISBN: 978-1-5043-6809-4 (hc)
ISBN: 978-1-5043-6811-7 (e)

Library of Congress Control Number: 2016916857

Balboa Press rev. date: 10/28/2016

FOR THE CHILDREN

CONTENTS

Step V — Sealing the Deal

INTRODUCTION

$\mathcal{M}$arriage is difficult. It is probably one of the hardest things most of us will ever attempt with our lives. After all, how many smart, successful people do you know who have gotten divorced or had a serious relationship fail?

The only thing most of us do that may be even harder than marriage is raising a child (as the parent of a 3-year-old, I swear medical school was easier), so of course, we try to do both at the same time. When you think about it, it is quite amazing that we don't have more divorces and messed-up kids than we do.

I'm not saying this to depress or scare you, but rather to help you approach your quest for marriage with the care and thoughtful attention it deserves. I also want to help you be gentle with yourself and to forgive yourself for any failed relationships in your past. You are in good company here if you have failed in a relationship or marriage or two.

The Problem with Following Your Heart

In your past relationships, you may have done what comes naturally, which is to follow your heart and go for the person you loved the most (or were most attracted to). You may have believed, as so many do, that if you loved each other enough, it would work out (as I did with my first marriage). When you discovered, like I did, that marriage takes a lot more than love, perhaps it left you wondering how your heart could be so wrong.

There's a good reason why you cannot trust your heart to make the decision all by itself. That's because your heart is essentially a slave to your feelings, and your feelings are the primary way your genes control you and make you do what they want. Yes, I'm talking about the genes you learned about in biology that are passed from generation to generation through our DNA.

Why would our genes want to control us? Because they have a single obsession: to reproduce themselves as many times as possible in the form of children who then can successfully pass the same genes on to their own children, generation after generation. Our genes don't care if we are happy or if we have satisfying marriages. They just want genetically fit offspring.

As a woman, that means your genes want you to reproduce with the most genetically fit male available; specifically, a dominant male who can fight to protect his children and has social standing and access to resources to provide for them as well. Your genes are far less concerned with his ability to be a good husband and don't care much if he is arrogant, addicted, manipulative, immature or even discretely unfaithful. (If this doesn't make sense, check out the full explanation in Appendix I.)

The Problem with Following Good Advice

After your initially passionate relationship with Mr. Dominant failed, maybe you tried the typical "marry your best friend" advice, or listened to your friends and family, who urged you to find someone with whom you share similar values and background. In other words, you were encouraged to seek compatibility or similarity, or some combination of the two.

Seems like good advice, doesn't it? Unfortunately, if you tried to follow their advice, you probably found out that such an approach doesn't work in the long term either (as I did with my second marriage). If you married your best friend, you may have gotten along, but the sex was at best "meh" and at worst — well, like having sex with your best friend. If you went for similar values and background, you may have been shocked at how much trouble you had getting along because he kept triggering you just like your parents do (and he didn't make your toes curl in bed, either).

Maybe things didn't blow up as fast as with Mr. Dominant, but your relationship still eventually went south with Mr. Compatible and Mr.

Similar. Kind of like fine sandpaper — the imperfect fit slowly wore you down until your soul was filled with quiet desperation.

Isn't that what marriage therapy is for, to fix these kinds of issues? Sadly, the truth is no, it can't. Marriage therapy can help you communicate better and help you resolve a disagreement or two if you get stuck, but the marriage still has to be fundamentally sound for it to work. Marriage therapy can fix the 20%, but you still have get the 80% right by marrying well in the first place.

I know this because I was a semester away from finishing a master's degree in counseling and marriage therapy before leaving to start medical school. Then as a child psychiatrist, I have treated hundreds of children and their families over the years, which has given me unfettered access to the inner workings of those marriages and the limited benefits of their marriage therapy. I also spent a small fortune on several excellent marriage therapists over the course of two failed marriages. The bottom line is that marriage therapy can only do so much, and it can't fix a poor choice of whom you marry.

Again, I'm not trying to depress or scare you here, but it's important to lay the problem out honestly and openly so we can examine it and devise a real solution.

What is the problem, in a nutshell? Basically, that marriage is so challenging you have to make a good choice of whom to marry to have a reasonable chance of success, which is further complicated by the fact that the common advice you've previously heard is either wrong or at best incomplete. Worse, the usual advice points you in the wrong direction, so luck and random chance end up determining whether your marriage succeeds or fails, rather than improving your odds.

The Solution for a Successful Marriage

The good news is that this book contains a step-by-step system that is both effective and simple enough for the average person to apply it without any advanced knowledge or training in any field. I will teach you everything you need to know to apply it. All you need is already in your hands, plus, depending on a few variables, maybe a free download or two you can get from my website.

My system has five steps that we will work through together to teach you how to attract and marry the man you are meant for. This customized system was carefully designed to attract the precise man who will fit with you and you alone, not just a "good enough" man or a decent man for a one-size-fits-all marriage. I'm talking about that one man who makes your heart sing and satisfies your soul like no other.

During the first step, we will focus on the specific steps necessary to ensure you are fully prepared to fulfill your quest for such a marriage. This step isn't so much about changing you as it is about laying the necessary foundation and helping you develop the optimal mindset to manifest your marriage. We will work through the seven critical questions you must answer to prepare yourself and then explore the secret of the most successful marriages, so you will have the necessary mindset to manifest the marriage you were meant for.

During the second step, I will show you how to immediately eliminate 50 percent of the men you may encounter. These are the guys who are just not capable of being successfully married or are so far from being ready that you can't afford to wait for them to catch up with you. In case you struggle in any of these areas (eating the marshmallow or attachment), I will show you the fastest and most efficient way to get back on track.

In the third step, we will get to the heart of my system — we will identify your relational style on two key personality spectrums and then, using my unique framework of four primary male archetypes (Athlete, Engineer, Film Director, and Artist), teach you how to identify and attract the kind of man that best complements your style. I will also teach you how to identify and avoid the "shadow archetypes" that can at first seem like the guy you want, but who in reality only mimics your complementary archetype so you can avoid him before he even gets close.

This step is incredibly powerful because it will enable you to attract the precise type of man you will get along with the best while still having plenty of chemistry to keep the home fires burning for decades to come. It will also discourage the wrong types of men from approaching you and allow you to quickly spot and avoid them if they insist upon trying. This step alone will save you from years of wasted time and untold heartbreak.

The neuroscience and psychology-based process I teach in the first three steps will get you looking in the right ballpark, but science has its limits and it can't tell you who is the precise man you are meant for. That level of precision is only attainable with the assistance of the omniscient intelligence of God, Spirit, the Universe, your higher power, whatever you want to call it.

In the fourth step, we will kick it up a notch and go beyond the limits of science, engaging Spirit to draw to you the precise man you were meant for, the one who will satisfy you at the deepest level. In this step, I will teach you specific techniques that will make the proverbial needle in the haystack come to you as if you had a giant magnet.

After you find him, you still have to get him to the altar and start your marriage off on the right foot. In the fifth and final step, I will show you the precise path to the altar based on his archetype. I will also show you how to use each phase of your relationship to test him to ensure he is the precise one you were meant for and to prepare him to be a great husband. In most cases, you will have a ring on your finger within a year of meeting him (and if you don't I'll show you exactly how to deal with him to maximize your odds of getting a ring).

Why You Should Listen to Me

Not long ago, I was twice divorced due to poor choices of whom to marry. Both times, I was sure I had met the One, only to have it blow up in my face, leaving me to pick up the tattered pieces of my life.

Yet despite my painful failures, I still dreamed of being married and raising a family. However, there was added pressure this time because each failed marriage had almost cost a decade. I had to get it right this time because I wasn't sure I had more than one last attempt in me.

However, this time the odds were in my favor, because unlike my first two marriages, I was an associate professor of both adult and child psychiatry, and had spent almost a decade studying and teaching about virtually every aspect of human behavior. I also had the unique perspective of having worked with hundreds of couples over that decade, which afforded me unparalleled access to the inner workings of their relationships, both good and bad.

I had another ace up my sleeve as well. I spent the last two decades studying energetic and spiritual healing practices, from prayer and meditation to acupuncture and Reiki to shamanism and other indigenous healing practices, which gave me a wide set of tools to energetically and spiritually manifest whatever I desired.

Single for the third time after my second divorce, knowing this might be my last shot at marriage, I brought everything I knew to bear on the challenge of finding the precise person I was meant for, from psychology to neuroscience to spirituality. But I didn't stop there, because I didn't want to leave anything to chance. I read everything I could get my hands on about dating, attraction, and relationships that might teach me something new. I even made friends with other singles who seemed to have mastered dating, hoping I could learn from them.

I tried virtually every technique for meeting new people, from joining churches and clubs to matchmaking services to meeting new women in bars and coffee shops. I even joined several online dating websites and went on dozens and dozens of first dates. Despite all that, it still took me 18 months to meet (and longer to marry) the woman I was meant for. I don't want to you think this is magic and doesn't require time and effort.

Not long after I met my wife, I started teaching these concepts to single friends and then friends of friends. I am a teacher at heart and I wanted other people to be able to have an amazing marriage just like mine. With the help of my students, I was able to refine all the concepts and techniques I used down to their most effective forms. We were also able to determine the best way to teach these techniques so someone without a background in psychology can learn and apply them easily.

Over the years, most of my students have succeeded in having the amazing relationship or marriage they were meant for when they put in the time and effort to consistently apply this system.

Karen was a 35-year old school teacher who was stuck in a destructive cycle of repeatedly breaking up and getting back together with the father of her young son. I helped her recognize how her ex was in the 50% of men who just aren't capable of being successfully married so she could finally break it off with him for good. Afterward, we used shamanic techniques to clear her energetic blocks around love and marriage and then attract the precise man she was meant for, a tall engineer with a school age daughter, in less than a year. At last report, they are deeply in love and thinking about having a baby.

Another student, Amanda, was separated from the father of her young son, but still lived in the same house with him because he wouldn't move out. She also couldn't bring herself to kick him out despite his not holding a steady job for years. Even though he was perfectly capable of working, he would find some problem with every job he got and quit. My system helped her see his narcissism clearly and recognize how he kept manipulating her into taking care of him.

I taught her how to resist his manipulation so she could finally get rid of him. We then identified the relational archetype that best complemented her style and within only a few months she had met a handsome guy of the right archetype with a young son and a great career. At last report, they were happily married with a beautiful house in a great neighborhood with good schools.

Who This Book Is For

While this system works for both men and women (with some simple modifications), it was too hard to cover both versions in a single book, so I wrote this book for women, first because women read more than men. If all goes well, I'll follow up in a year or two with a version for men, but this is a book for women looking to marry men.

This book is also only for women who want a monogamous marriage to a man. This is not a dating book to help you get a hot date for this weekend. Nor is it a book on finding the perfect man for an open marriage. It also wasn't written for same-sex marriages. Even though some parts may apply there are still critical differences in the dynamic between same-sex couples compared to heterosexual couples and my system is not designed to address those.

This book is for a wide range of ages. It can be used (with a few caveats) by women as young as 20. At the upper end, the oldest female student that has successfully used my system was in her late 50s, but I don't see why a woman in her 60s or even older couldn't be successful with it as well.

Finally, this book is for singles only. It is not about fixing your marriage. Please go to marriage therapy for that. I know I said earlier that marriage therapy can only fix the 20%, but sometimes a problem can seem huge and overwhelming when actually it is fairly straightforward to fix. So please give your marriage every chance to succeed by doing whatever you can to save it. Otherwise you may be haunted by what ifs.

How to Use this Book

This book was designed and written to teach you step by step how to attract and marry the man you were meant for. The steps are presented in a specific order, and in a couple of chapters you will be asked to complete quizzes, which will then determine the path you need to follow for the rest of the book. Please do the quizzes as you get to them and then only read the chapters you are directed to read. I know you'll be tempted to read the other chapters, but at first I am asking you not to, because you will risk getting confused and misapplying something meant for a different person. If you must read them, at least wait until you've mastered your customized approach first.

Since this book was written in a step by step fashion, you can actually use this book like a workbook were you only work on one step at a time. It is perfectly acceptable to read a chapter and complete the tasks in it before reading the next chapter. In fact, I would encourage you to resist the urge to read this book through and instead work chapter by chapter.

I also recommend waiting to start applying this system until you have at least completed step 3 because the first three steps have to be used together in order to be effective. However, it would be even better to complete step 4 before you start applying the system. Step 5 on the other hand is for after you have started dating a man who might be the one and you can wait until then to read that section.

You may want to work through this book with a single friend who also wants to get married (and meets the criteria in Chapter One to ensure she is ready, which is critical for both of you, as you will soon see). Just like having a workout buddy to support and motivate you at the gym, having a companion on this journey will increase your odds of success. You'll be able to support each other, share objective feedback (sometimes it is hard to see things in ourselves that are obvious to others) and encourage each other to stick to the system and go on one more first date even when you don't feel like talking to anyone.

Dating is emotionally hard and takes lots of energy, so that little push and encouragement from your buddy could make all the difference between finding your husband sooner rather than later or not at all.

Finally, I am always available for questions and support through my website (www.scottcarrollmd.com). In addition to getting your questions answered, you can also sign up to receive encouraging weekly e-mails and to read helpful articles on related topics like fitness and navigating the online dating world. You can even download online dating guides that specifically address how to attract your complementary archetype online.

Just know as you begin this journey that you are not alone because Spirit loves you and longs to bring you the amazing marriage you seek. You will see evidence of that support in the little coincidences that steer you on your way and in the subtle hints that you have met the one meant for you. As you begin this journey, trust that you will be guided to him and that all things work together for your highest good.

Blessings,
Scott Carroll, MD

STEP I

Preparing Yourself for Marriage

CHAPTER ONE

Are You Ready for Marriage?

*T*he first step in my system is to prepare yourself for marriage. While this topic might seem a bit dull, it is critical to ensuring your future success. You wouldn't build a house on an unstable foundation, would you? We are doing the same thing here: building a solid foundation for your marriage.

To that end, please work through these seven questions to ensure you are ready to take the next step in attracting the man you are meant for. It may take some time to address all of the issues raised in these questions, but it will be time well spent because it will prepare you optimally to be married and use this system. I urge you to complete each question fully before you continue.

1. **Why do you want to be married?** It seems like such a simple question, but simply wanting to be married is no longer a good enough reason to get married in our modern society. Yes, there was a time, not that long ago, when being single severely limited and hampered your life, but today marriage really is a choice and not a necessity. However, the true reasons why we desire things are often not clear to our conscious minds, so find a quiet spot and give yourself several minutes in the silence to see what bubbles up from deep inside you.

Don't judge the answers that come up, because you need to be honest with yourself here. Just write them all down as they come up. Continue to quietly contemplate the question until no new answers have come up for several minutes. Afterward, look over your answers.

Healthy reasons for wanting to be married include things like seeking companionship, raising a family, or sharing some purpose together. The list of healthy reasons is long and varied, so we'll be spending much of the next chapter exploring them. For now, we just need to make sure you don't want to be married for an *unhealthy* reason.

Similar to the list of healthy reasons, the full list of *unhealthy* reasons is quite long as well, but the one thing they have in common is that they use marriage to solve a problem that is better solved by other means. For example, maybe you want to live a luxurious lifestyle. While marrying someone with good financial prospects might be smart, marrying someone just for their money isn't usually the start to a great marriage. After all, how much money does it take to stay married to someone if you can't stand being touched by him and if you can't be with whom you truly love?

Other examples include things like getting out of debt, moving out of your parents' home, or even getting out of your small town. While those things may happen as a result of a good marriage, it is generally better to accomplish these things on your own before you get married. The ironic truth of marriage is that the less you need to be married, the better your marriage tends to be.

Spend some time with your list of reasons to see if each reason can be satisfied by another means. If a reason can be satisfied by another means, commit to satisfying it by that non-marriage means.

If you want a luxurious life style, figure out how to start your own business or become successful in a lucrative profession. Similarly, if you need to get out of debt, learn how to budget and be frugal so you can do so quickly. If you want get out of your small town, start looking at job prospects in larger cities. If you satisfy those desires on your own you won't end up burdening your marriage with them.

2. **Are you ready for monogamy?** Unfaithfulness will destroy a marriage faster than almost anything else. Marriage means having sex with the same person for possibly longer than you've been alive.

Not everyone is cut out for that level of sameness and repetition. Could you stand going to the same restaurant for the rest of your life? You will always get the best seat and you will never need a reservation. You can also have anything you want on the menu and you can even work with the chef to change the menu from time to time — but you can never step foot in another restaurant, ever, no matter how amazing it may seem.

If you can honestly say you would be happy living that way, then you are ready for marriage.

3. **Are you really single?** Many people start trying to meet the next person before they have actually broken up with the last one. Don't test the waters like that. It is both dishonest and bad dating karma. Ask yourself if there is someone who thinks they are still in an exclusive relationship with you (if you have served them with a restraining order, that's good enough)?

Sit them down (in a public place, if you think they will take it badly) and tell them in no uncertain terms that your relationship is over. If you need help with telling them it's over, you can read about how to do it with class on my website (http://www.scottcarrollmd.com/saying-no-with-class/).

Similarly, do you tend to have your next boyfriend lined up, ready to go the minute you break up with your current boyfriend? Many women keep a waitlist of potential boyfriends. The problem with this is that quality men don't tend to put up with being waitlisted and you risk settling for a waitlist guy simply because he's available and you don't like to be alone.

Lose the waitlist and learn to tolerate being alone. It just takes a little practice and you can start by using your new free time to read this book and work on the exercises in it. Plus, being comfortable being alone is a wonderful gift, because it allows you to know yourself and to only be with a man because you truly enjoy being with him, not because you are uncomfortable being alone. However, if being alone makes you excessively anxious or depressed, you probably need to see a psychotherapist about it (See Appendix 2 for details on how to find one).

Another problem I occasionally see with my students is someone who is still living with their ex, usually for financial reasons. I get it, but do you think a quality man is going to want to date you if you are still living with your ex? No, he's not, because the last thing he wants to do is to star in your reality TV show. Plus, you'll probably never convince him that things are completely over and platonic with your ex.

Heck, have you even convinced yourself that it's completely over, that no part of you hopes he will turn it around and be the man you originally thought he was? If one of you just can't move out, either some part of you hopes you'll get back together or one of you is a mooch. If he's the mooch, let him mooch off his mother or another family member. However, if you are the one who can't afford to move out, start looking for other roommates, apply for better-paying jobs, and do whatever it takes to get your financial house in order before you focus on getting married.

Finally, are you still sleeping with anyone (that includes any form of sex, fooling around, or cuddling), including with your ex? Many former couples hook up, which is generally harmless, but it won't serve you if your goal is to attract an awesome husband. As I said before, a quality man won't believe that things are completely over with your ex if you still get together. Cut it off so you can start fresh with a blank sheet of paper.

Similarly, having regular sex with anyone who isn't the one won't serve your quest for an awesome marriage, because regular sex puts you at risk of becoming biochemically bonded to your partner, similar to what happens in addiction. Just as with an addiction, it can cloud your mind and induce you to make a poor choice in terms of whom to marry. If you need sex, a side hookup is fine; just don't let it turn into a regular occurrence. How likely is it that a quality man will believe that your regular sex is completely casual?

4. **Are you financially stable?** Notice that I didn't say rich. Instead, what I mean is that you have a reliable source of income, you spend less than you make, and you are not overwhelmed with debt. If you are struggling with any of these financial issues, you need to deal with that before you focus on getting married. Financial

problems are one of the most common reasons couples fight and a major cause of divorce. Why would you want to burden your marriage from the beginning with these problems? Plus, quality men tend to be sensitive to how a woman manages her money and don't want to marry women who are bad with money and will drag them down.

Now is also a good time to run your credit report and get it cleaned up, because it is not fair to bring a bad credit score to a new marriage. When you marry someone, your financial and credit histories become combined over time, and the lower credit score tends to pull down the good score. Also, there are many advantages to having a good credit score, because it allows you to pay less for all kinds of things, from insurance to negotiating a better price for a car, not just get lower interest rates.

You will also need to set aside a little extra money each month for dating. While dating doesn't have to be expensive, it's not completely free, either. For example, you'll need to pay for a membership to at least one online dating website (the free ones are full of people who aren't serious about a relationship or can't afford to pay for a membership). You'll also need some nice clothing and be able to afford coffee/drinks when you go on a date.

5. **Are you emotionally stable?** All of us get nervous or sad from time to time, but are your emotions significantly interfering with your life? Do you get so anxious that you can't do certain things or can't relax and enjoy yourself? Maybe you struggle with sadness or low energy and motivation to the point that it affects your job or relationships? If so, you will need to get these emotions under control before you start dating, because they will limit your ability to date, scare off quality men, and be a burden on your marriage.

If you are still grieving some loss, such as your last relationship, you need to finish your grieving process before starting to date. Trust me, it is really embarrassing if you burst out in tears during a date because of something he said or did that reminded you of your ex.

The best way for most people to address these issues is to go to individual psychotherapy. Medication may work faster, but it only works when you take it and can have annoying side effects, especially sexual ones. In contrast, the benefits of psychotherapy can last a lifetime. Therapists also make excellent sounding boards as you go through the dating process. See Appendix II for tips on finding a therapist.

6. **Are you sober?** Addiction and marriage are inherently incompatible. Marriage is hard enough without adding the burden of an addiction. Alcohol and drugs also cloud the mind and interfere with making good choices in terms of whom you date and marry. Furthermore, quality men are going to reject you if you have an alcohol or drug problem. Only men with low standards or who have a problem themselves will overlook yours.

Let's go beyond addiction for a moment. If you drink alcohol daily, even if it is just a glass or two, or if you get drunk most weekends, I would recommend that you cut back before you start dating. Daily drinking and regular benders are bad for your health. Do you really want a marriage that revolves around drinking and getting drunk? Even if you manage to marry a man who doesn't have an alcohol problem now, why run the risk of either of you developing a problem?

Similarly, if you use marijuana illegally or regularly, you will need to cut back as well. Many quality men have jobs and careers that would be at risk if an illegal activity were going on in their homes.

Even if you live somewhere it is legal, marijuana still can make you lazy and unmotivated. Quality men who are serious about their careers aren't lazy and don't want to be with someone who is lazy, either.

Of course, if you use any hard drugs at all, you absolutely need to stop and get professional help before you consider dating. Hard drugs are dangerous and extremely addicting as well as illegal. If you have any doubts about how dangerous or addicting they are, spend a night working in the emergency room of any large hospital in a major city. You will see exactly what I'm talking about. Just be aware that it typically takes professional help and strong support to beat a drug problem.

7. **Are you at least 23 years old?** I say this because your brain will not be fully developed and neurologically mature until you are 23 at the earliest (or as late as 25, which is the earliest the male brain typically matures). This has nothing to do with intelligence or education, but with the fact that your frontal lobes, which are responsible for rational thought and objective judgment, are not fully developed until then. Before your frontal lobes finish their development, your judgment is susceptible to being overwhelmed by your emotions and is a major cause of "Shiny Object Syndrome" and "Dating ADD." Why do you think car insurance rates drop so much when you turn 25?

If you are under 23, you can read this book and start working on attracting the ideal man to marry, but please wait until you are at least 23 (or 25 to be even safer) to actually marry him. You need your brain to be fully developed to be sure he meets all the necessary criteria to be the one you are meant for and to prevent your judgment from being clouded because you are love-drunk.

In Review

- Why do you want to be married?
- Are you ready for monogamy?
- Are you really single?
- Are you financially stable?
- Are you emotionally stable?
- Are you sober?
- Are you at least 23 years old?

CHAPTER TWO

The Secret to a Satisfying Marriage

*N*otice that this chapter is titled "The Secret to a Satisfying Marriage" and not "The Secret to a Happy Marriage." We often say we want to be happy, where happiness equates to a blissful state of constant joy, untroubled by struggle, challenge, or hard work. But when is anything worthwhile in life or marriage ever free from struggle and hard work, especially when struggle and hard work are often the sources of our joy?

I think a better, more realistic goal for both life and marriage is satisfaction, because hard work, struggle, and challenges are both inevitable and a source of our joy. Yes, we have moments where we are briefly free from struggle and are thus at peace, but the peace quickly turns into boredom and apathy if a new struggle doesn't present itself. In fact, are we not most happy when we have triumphed over some great challenge?

Happiness is such an ephemeral thing that is here one moment and gone the next, that trying to be happy is almost like chasing the wind. However, you merely have to look back over your accomplishments and how you have lived and loved to be satisfied – which will then make you happy. That is why seeking satisfaction rather than happiness in both life and marriage is a more certain path to the happiness we all desire.

What is the secret to a satisfying marriage? Being in love is clearly not the answer. Virtually every newlywed couple loves each other, but still nearly half end up divorcing, while many more suffer in poor marriages.

Similarly, sustaining sexual attraction is not the secret, either. Many divorced couples quietly hook up for sex years after divorcing, which shows that the sexual attraction wasn't gone just that it couldn't save the marriage. In addition, all the information we have gained about sex over the last few decades has done little to bring down our divorce rate.

Don't get me wrong: Love is clearly important. After all, why would you marry someone you didn't love? Love is necessary, but it is not sufficient in and of itself to ensure a successful marriage. The same can be said for sexual attraction. It is clearly necessary, but it is not sufficient, either. Something else is required.

What about communication? The marriage therapy industry would have us believe that, if we could only communicate better, our marital problems would be solved. However, after spending a small fortune on some excellent therapists over the course of two marriages, I can assure you that no amount of improved communication can overcome a poor choice of whom to marry. Again, good communication is necessary, but it is not the secret.

What about compatibility and companionship? That must be the secret, right? Well, if it was, I would just tell you to go marry your best male friend because you get along so well. You'll probably continue to get along well, but could you stand having sex only with him for the rest your life? Again, both are obviously important, but not the secret.

Sharing a Purpose, Sharing a Life

Are you ready for the big secret? Here it is.

The great secret to a successful, satisfying marriage is a strongly shared purpose you are both passionate about and committed to — an overriding goal both of you share that can be the glue that holds you together and motivates you to work hard to overcome the endless challenges every marriage faces.

You still need all the other pieces — from love and great sex to communication and companionship — but a strong, shared purpose is the glue that holds them together, much like mortar holds bricks together to form a wall. When the bricks start to crumple, a strong purpose can hold your marriage together, allowing you to repair the broken parts before the wall collapses and divorce becomes inevitable.

Let me give you some examples to clarify what I mean. One of the most common shared purposes of satisfying marriages is to have children and raise a family together. Other examples include building a business or being deeply committed to helping the less fortunate. It can even be something as simple as a shared passion for traveling or, for one couple I know, raising show dogs.

The reason why a shared purpose is the secret is because purpose is so incredibly powerful. The famous existential psychologist and author of Man's Search for Meaning, Victor Frankl, discovered this when he was sent to a concentration camp by the Nazis in World War II for being Jewish. While at the camp, he observed that it was not necessarily the strong, the young, or the healthy who survived. It was the people with an all-consuming, overriding purpose who survived, despite being elderly, sick, or alone.

Frankl also recognized that it didn't matter what the purpose was — only that it was strongly held. It could be anything from wanting to live to see family again or to make a particularly cruel guard be held accountable.

Similarly, when a marriage has a shared purpose that you are both passionate about and committed to, it allows the couple to shift their focus from how they are getting along in any given moment to something more important. As a result, the couple is focused on the long journey, rather than on every little bump in the road. A strongly shared purpose also motivates you to work out your differences and to compromise so you can keep working together, rather than focus on who's right and who's wrong.

Another benefit of a strongly shared purpose is as a source of joy and satisfaction in a marriage. For example, if your shared purpose is to raise a family, your children's growth and accomplishments are a source of joy and satisfaction. Similarly, if you are building a business together, its growth and success becomes a source of joy and satisfaction. Travel, helping others, collecting art, raising show dogs — whatever your purpose is, has the potential to be a source of joy and satisfaction that can sustain a marriage.

The importance of having a strongly shared purpose as a source of joy and satisfaction for sustaining a marriage has to do with a little molecule called oxytocin. Oxytocin is the hormone in our brains that causes all those goopy feelings of love. It also controls our emotional bonds to friends and family. A large body of research shows that oxytocin levels spike early in a romantic relationship and then remain high for the next few years.

However, over the next five to seven years together, our oxytocin level drops almost all the way down to where it was before we met our partner. This is why many evolutionary biologists believe that humans are designed for serial monogamy rather than life-long unions — five to seven years is about the time it takes for a couple to get pregnant and raise one or two children to the point that the children are old enough to be weaned and be raised by either parent alone when they separate.

I know five to seven years seems really short and there are some things you can do to temporarily boost the oxytocin levels, like romantic getaways and frequent sex, but the increase is nowhere close to what meeting a new lover causes. This waning of attraction is inevitable for couples. That is why having a strongly shared purpose helps the couple survive the seven-year itch. It keeps them focused on the goals of their marriage and gives them a source of joy and satisfaction to help resist the temptation caused by their brains being flooded with oxytocin from meeting someone new.

The other benefit of a shared purpose is that it motivates you to compromise. If you have never been married (living together is not the same and doesn't count), you probably don't realize how much two people can get on each other's nerves. What initially seemed like a cute little quirk when you were dating often turns into a major annoyance once you are constantly living together. Not surprisingly, if you don't compromise and work through those annoyances, they lead to resentment, which causes your oxytocin level to drop even faster.

I mentioned a few common purposes, but your purpose really can be almost anything. I know one couple that raises horses together. I know another couple that started a small foundation that provides aid and assistance after natural disasters around the world. Many couples I know love the outdoors and go camping and hiking together every opportunity they get. A few I know live near a ski area so they can ski whenever they are not working.

Again, it almost doesn't matter what the purpose is, just that it is shared and you are both committed to and passionate about it.

My wife and I have two purposes (yes, you can have more than one). First, we wanted to have a child and raise a small family together. Even before I met my wife, I knew I wanted a family, and I let her know my desire early on, while we were dating. At first, she was unsure because she had let go of the idea of being a mom during the struggles of her first marriage, but once she got to see how well we worked as a couple, she quickly warmed to the idea and was eager to start a family as soon as we were married. Now she loves being a mom more than she ever imagined.

Our second purpose is a combination of our two long-held dreams that go back many years before we met. My wife had long dreamed of doing health and wellness coaching, while I dreamed of public speaking and leading and teaching workshops. We have now combined our dreams and we're developing workshops where she does the one-on-one coaching and I speak and teach the group.

Having a second purpose is critically important for us because eventually, our daughter will grow up and move out into the world to create her own life. After that, our role as parents will diminish to the point that it will no longer be effective at organizing and aligning our marriage. In contrast, our health and wellness work may be starting to hit its stride at that point.

Many couples face this problem. They work well as parents together, but the lack of a backup purpose becomes apparent once all of their children grow up and move out. That is why so many couples divorce shortly after the last child has moved out. Even if they don't divorce, they often start living parallel lives where they barely interact.

Parallel lives may work for a while, but eventually one of them meets someone else they can't resist and has an affair. That is why I strongly recommend that you and your husband have at least one purpose other than raising a family.

Uncovering Your Purpose For Marriage

The key is to know your purpose or purposes before you even start dating. After all, you don't want to figure out after you are married that your husband loves to travel and you are more of a homebody. Even worse, you may be focused on raising a family while he is putting in so many hours at work building his career that you start feeling like a single mom.

Yes, you may find out that you share his passion after you are married, but you also might not. Why take that risk if you don't have to?

Take a moment to think about what can serve as your purpose. A big clue comes from your dreams for your life. Put this book down and take a few minutes to sit in the silence and see what comes up. Write down everything that pops into your head without judging it, no matter how outrageous it seems. Don't worry if you have no idea of how to manifest your dreams or if you don't think you could ever accomplish them.

Now look at each dream and imagine not having accomplished it as you lie on your deathbed. Which dream causes the greatest amount of pain as you imagine never accomplishing it? Which causes the next-greatest amount of pain? Rank each dream by the amount of pain it causes. The amount of pain you feel lets you know what is most important to you at the deepest level.

After you have ranked your list, sit in the silence again to see what bubbles up about the list. Do you need to switch items or add something? Next, consider whether each dream is compatible with being married. If your top two or three dreams are not compatible with being married (such as if you feel a calling to become a nun), you may need to reconsider your desire to be married.

If your top dream is raising a family, you have picked one of the best reasons to be married, but as I mentioned earlier, you will need a backup for when the kids grow up and leave the nest. While you can always change your purpose later, you should go into your marriage with at least one backup ready to go. In fact, every marriage needs at least one backup purpose, in case the primary purpose ever fades or weakens for some reason.

Once you have identified your top two or three purposes for marriage, you will be ready when you start dating.

In Review

- Satisfaction is a more sustainable and achievable goal in marriage than constant happiness and bliss.

- Love, sexual attraction, communication, compatibility, and companionship are necessary, but are not the secrets to a satisfying marriage.
- Having a strong purpose (or two or three) is the secret to a satisfying marriage because it will hold you together through the seven-year itch and other rough times.
- You need more than one purpose, especially if your main one is to raise a family, because you need a backup for when the kids grow up and move out.

STEP II

Is He Husband Material?

CHAPTER THREE

Did He Eat the Marshmallow?

Let's start with the single most important skill in relationships, as well as in life: the ability to delay gratification.

A series of experiments at Stanford in the late 1960s and early 1970s called the Marshmallow Experiments demonstrated how important it is to be able to delay gratification. In these experiments, four-year-old children were given marshmallows or some other treat and were told that if they didn't eat the marshmallow for 15 minutes, they would get a second marshmallow.

Approximately a third of the four-year-olds managed to resist eating the marshmallow. The children were then followed for more than 20 years until they were young adults — and the results were striking. The children who didn't eat the marshmallow had higher SAT scores and better grades, were more successful in their careers, had better relationships, were less likely to have divorced, and were happier in general.

The children who ate the marshmallow didn't fare as well on average. Many struggled and had a variety of problems, including criminal charges and poor academics with lower grades and higher rates of failing and dropping out of school. They were also less happy, had more drug and alcohol problems, and were less successful in their relationships.

On the positive side, some of the children who ate the marshmallow did develop the ability to delay gratification over the next few years, which enabled them to be successful like the non-eaters, but even when you added them to the non-eaters, they only added up to about half of the children tested.

These experiments have been replicated in other countries and cultures, with similar results and were independent of intelligence or family background.

What these experiments demonstrate is that the ability to delay gratification is either innate or develops early in life and that it is a critical skill for being successful in modern society across a broad range of areas, from education and careers to health and relationships. In addition, the effect of the ability to delay gratification is not just a result of having a high IQ or being raised by a good family. Furthermore, replicating the studies across many cultures and countries indicates that the ability to delay gratification is a universal condition common to all humans.

What this means for you and your quest for a successful and satisfying marriage is that you are far better off marrying a man with the ability to delay gratification who wouldn't have eaten the marshmallow. How do you tell if someone ate the marshmallow or not, so to speak, besides asking his mother or inventing a time machine? There are three things to look at that will clearly tell you if he ate the marshmallow or not.

The True Meaning of His Credit Score

A credit score is the adult equivalent of the marshmallow test. Think about it: To have a high credit score, you have to repetitively resist the urge to buy things on credit or, if you do use credit, pay your bills on time and only have a reasonable amount of good debt in the form of a low home mortgage, modest student loans, a low car payment, and no carried balances on your credit cards.

This is not just about being frugal; it is about resisting temptation from new credit card offers to not buying a bigger house just because you get a raise to resisting the urge to buy a nicer car just because you qualify for bigger loan.

Of course, the one exception is if you have literally never had any debt in your life because you have always paid cash for everything; you will have a falsely low credit score because of a lack of data. That is why you have to at least borrow a little bit or have a credit card you use to have a meaningful score. Just know that if a man has the self-discipline to always pay cash that he legally earned and never take out payday loans or title loans, or pawn things, he didn't eat the marshmallow.

Beyond being a sign of the ability to delay gratification, credit scores can tell you a lot about a man.

Greater than 800

He's a supersaver. He lives well below his means and is serious about saving. In fact, you may need to see if he can loosen up a bit so you can actually live in a decent house and take a nice vacation occasionally. If you have a high credit score as well (> 750), just know that you will be millionaires and live in a shack ... but your children will have an awesome inheritance, so start setting up the trust fund now. If you have a low to moderate credit score (less than 750), you will probably have to get better with money if you want your marriage to work because he is not the compromising type, at least when it comes to money.

Guys with credit scores of over 800 are rare and a bit unusual. They often live very frugally. They buy the cheapest items that will get the job done and will use those items until they literally fall apart and can't be fixed anymore. They may also be a bit of a hoarder and have trouble throwing something away, even if it's broken or useless and taking up space. They can also have unusual lifestyles, like not owning a car even though they live in the suburbs or standard items like a washer and dryer or a TV.

They may also have strange money-making ideas, like a guy I know who bought a rundown house on the edge of a ghetto to live in and fix up to flip, even though he was in law school. Alternatively, he may just be committed to a financial goal such as saving enough money so he can retire early and then travel or start his own business.

The bottom line is you need to get to know this type of man well and make sure you can handle his approach to life and money, because this is one cat you're not going to be able to change.

750 to 800

He's a saver, but he has a nice balance between saving and having fun. He will actually take you to nice restaurants and on nice vacations. He also won't make you drive a 10-year-old bucket after you are married. He may drive a 10-year-old bucket, but then he knows how to fix it if it breaks down.

If your credit score is higher than his, he may be good for you and help you loosen up a bit and have more fun while still meeting your financial goals. If your scores are the same, good for you, because you will probably do well around money issues since you're balanced. If your score is lower and you're not still in school, he will be good for you in terms of helping you live within your means and save for retirement. These guys make good husbands because they can balance having fun with being prepared for the future.

700 to 750

He's okay with money and credit, but he leans to the fun side and could do a little better in terms of saving and living within his means. If your credit score is greater than 750, you need to make sure he is open to being a little more responsible and willing to follow your lead, at least when it comes to financial decisions.

This was the situation I was in when I met my wife. My score was in the low 700s while hers was in the high 700s. Even though I made a lot more money than she did, I was not as careful with my spending. I was enjoying my lifestyle as a single doctor — throwing fancy parties, eating at fine restaurants, and driving a sports car, while she was working her way through graduate school so she didn't have to take out student loans.

I have wisely followed her example in our marriage when it comes to money. While I'm good about major expenses like the mortgage, cars, and investing, my eyes glaze over when it comes to budgeting and smaller purchases. On the other hand, she likes to budget and find the best deals on everyday purchases. Since we play to each other's strengths, we are in good shape for retirement and with saving for our daughter's education.

If both of you have credit scores in the low 700s, you will need to work on managing your money a bit better. If your score is below 700 and his is only in the low 700s, you will need to do some serious work on controlling your spending and educating yourself about managing your money. I would recommend starting with Suze Orman's book, *The Money Book for the Young, Fabulous and Broke*, since she wrote it for younger people who are early in their careers and need to learn basic money management skills, as opposed to most financial books that target those about to retire.

Less than 700

This guy has serious issues with money — serious enough that you don't want marry him until he gets his score up over 700. Furthermore, he has to be actively working on improving his score and you need to see a positive trend upwards. Otherwise, walk away because he is not husband material and will put your financial future at grave risk if you marry him.

The reason is that when it comes to marriage, both of you have to be good with money because it is far easier for him to pull you down than it is for you to pull him up. When you are married, your credit also tends to become intertwined over time, no matter how much you may try to keep it separate. It only takes one joint purchase or rental agreement to link your credit scores for years to come — and getting divorced does nothing to separate your credit.

That is because creditors don't care what your divorce decree says about who is supposed to pay which debt. As a result, it is not unusual for one person to have to pay off all of their ex's debts from during (and even before) the marriage to repair their own credit score. Ask yourself, do you literally want to pay for his financial sins?

Poor money management and money problems have probably destroyed almost as many marriages as infidelity. You will have enough arguments and disagreements about finances even if you are both good with money, so why set yourself up for even more conflict? You wouldn't marry a guy with a long history of cheating, so why would you marry a guy with a long history of overspending, excessive debt, and living above his means?

Health and Fitness for the Long Run

The next area where the inability to delay gratification on a sustained basis shows up is with health and fitness.

Similar to credit scores, health and fitness also have a major impact on a marriage. Most illnesses these days are due to unhealthy lifestyles rather than aging or bad luck, and are almost entirely preventable. Health care is also extremely expensive, and a major illness can wipe you out financially, even if you have good health insurance, because of all the co-pays and non-covered expenses.

Men are actually more vulnerable to poor health choices than women and routinely die young or become disabled well before retirement age if they don't work hard to take care of their health. In fact, so many men with unhealthy life styles die in their 60s and 70s (and even 50s) that an 80-year-old man has a better chance of living another 15 years than a 60-year-old man does. Unless you literally want to be your bed-ridden husband's nurse while your friends are all enjoying their active retirements, you need to marry a man with good health habits.

You need to look at three areas of health in a man to ensure he is "fit" for marriage: 1) substance use, which includes smoking, alcohol, and drugs; 2) diet and exercise; and 3) body shape. Including substance use on this list is probably obvious. Since there are some twists here that may surprise you, let's get the obvious stuff out of the way quickly so we can get on to the more interesting parts.

Substance Use (and Abuse)

Of course, smoking is extremely lethal and every puff is like inhaling death into your body. It is essentially a slow form of suicide. Why would you want to marry someone who was committing suicide in front of you? That said, many people get addicted to smoking when they are young, before they fully grasp how addicting and deadly it is. Maybe that is what happened to you. If so, you need to make your health a top priority.

If you need to quit, get on nicotine replacement with patches and gum, and go to any free smoking-cessation classes or support groups in your area. If that doesn't work, see your doctor, because there are medications that can reduce your cravings and help you quit. Also, recognize that the average former smoker had to try eight or nine times before succeeding in quitting.

You also should expect your husband to have stopped smoking for at least a year before you marry him. However, it is better to marry a guy who has never smoked. Even though it only takes six months for his heart attack risk to return to normal, it takes more than 15 years for his risk of lung and other cancers to come down (they never completely go back to normal). In addition, secondhand smoke causes all manner of health problems in children and almost half of all lung cancers.

I know e-cigarettes (vaping) are a popular alternative to smoking nowadays, and the initial research suggests that they are not as dangerous as cigarettes and can help people stop smoking, but their long-term health risks are still unclear. There is significant concern among health experts that the other chemicals in the e-liquid, especially propylene glycol and glycerin, combine to produce toxins when they are heated. My take is that completely quitting is preferable, while vaping is the lesser evil.

Alcohol use is the next big danger. While small amounts of alcohol daily (one to two beers, glasses of wine or shots of liquor per day) seem beneficial, the benefit is actually caused by helping with stress (except for the resveratrol found in red wine and, to a lesser degree, in white wine). However, exercise and other stress reduction techniques are far more effective and better for your health. It is also hard to have only one or two drinks without sliding into heavier use when life inevitably gets tough or stressful. That is why I recommend staying away from anyone who drinks daily.

As for the weekend drinker, there is strong scientific evidence that five or more drinks (four drinks for women) in a single day in a month is associated with future alcohol addiction and with serious health risks on its own. New research has also shown that heavy drinking in early adulthood significantly increases early onset dementia in males in their 50s and 60s, so you should also stay away from anyone who likes to party more than a few times a year.

Let's talk about marijuana and other "legal drugs" for a moment. Marijuana is legal in some states already and may soon be legal nationwide. However, even in states where it is legal, employers still have the right to test and fire employees for marijuana use. Regular use also causes a condition known as Amotivational Syndrome.

The name says it all: Marijuana can make you fat and lazy. Why do you want to marry a guy who is fat and lazy, and can be fired at any moment because getting high is more important to him than doing the best he can for his family? Enough said.

Similarly, using "spice" or "wax" and other synthetic or concentrated forms of marijuana are also a bad idea. While only some forms are illegal, they are actually far more dangerous than marijuana. They can be up to 800 times stronger and can cause serious psychiatric problems, such as paranoia, delusions, and hallucinations that can last for months and even years even after someone stops using them. Be smart and stay away from it and anyone who uses it.

As for the illegal drugs, you should be able to guess my answer by now. Even occasional use that seems harmless is still an example of eating the marshmallow. Again, do you really want to married to a guy who can get fired from his job because of a surprise drug test, or even thrown in jail because partying is more important to him than taking care of his family?

Diet and Exercise

Now let's take a look at diet and exercise. Having good genes can cover up all manner of poor behavior for a while, but over time, habitual behavior will take over and determine a guy's level of health. Don't be fooled by how good he looks; pay attention to how he takes care of himself. Does he at least attempt to eat a balanced diet with occasional salads and green vegetables? Or is his idea of a vegetable corn on the cob, mashed potatoes, or French fries?

Similarly, if his idea of exercise is doing "12-ounce curls" while walking back to the couch from the fridge, you may have a problem. Being sedentary is just as lethal for a man as drinking or smoking. He doesn't have to be super-fit with six-pack abs, but he does need to exercise regularly. If he could stand to be more active, invite him to join you when you exercise. He may get into it, and you'll get both hotter and healthier.

You can at least take long walks in the park if he won't go for normal exercise. Being around nature is great for reducing stress and you will have plenty of time to talk and bond.

Body Shape

Finally, let's talk about body shape. Notice I said body shape rather than weight. That is because weight doesn't correlate with health very much. Muscle weighs more than fat, and where you store your fat makes a big difference, too. Fat just underneath the skin that hides muscle definition (think football linemen versus wide receivers) is actually fairly harmless from a health standpoint.

However, fat inside the belly is extremely dangerous because it causes high blood pressure, high cholesterol, and diabetes, and leads to heart attacks and strokes. Being a bit round and soft may not be as dangerous as being skinny with a belly that makes you look a bit pregnant. In fact, these skinny "pregnant" guys routinely have worse problems with high cholesterol, high blood pressure, and diabetes, and have more heart attacks and strokes, than the guy who is a little fat all over.

When you meet a new guy, look at how much his belly sticks out. It is a better gauge of his health than his weight or even his body fat percentage.

Getting on Track with His Potential

The third marshmallow test has to do with career and education. Basically, you want to see if he is on track to building a stable career so he can support a family (unless you plan to take care of that yourself). Over the years, I have met dozens and dozens of women who have lamented about how much potential their ex-husbands had yet never lived up to. The ex-husbands were talented, but due to a variety of factors (from laziness to liking pot too much, to getting easily bored), they either never finished their education or never developed their careers.

I'm not saying you have to be with a man with multiple advanced degrees; he just needs to have a marketable skill to build a successful career or business on. Besides, some guys stay in school getting degrees to avoid working, and many advanced degrees lead to careers that don't pay very well. Plumbers and electricians routinely make more than college professors because they have valuable skills and can demand top dollar.

One of my buddies is a great example of this. He doesn't have a college degree, but he's smart and hard-working, and knows more about designing and constructing buildings than many engineers. As a result, large construction companies hire him to lead teams to build complicated things like hospitals. In fact, he was recently promoted to vice president of a large nationwide construction company because he's that good.

What you're looking for is a guy who is either well on his way to establishing a successful career or is at least working hard to get the training or education he needs to be successful. The key is that he is committed to putting in the time and hard work it takes to be excellent at what he does. It has long been noted that the top 20 percent in every career field are so in demand that they are rarely unemployed and even then, don't stay unemployed for long.

Also, if a guy is still in school or training, make sure he isn't racking up too much student loan debt. A good rule of thumb is to only borrow as much as you can earn in one year working in that career. For example, a medical student may borrow $200,000 to go to medical school, but if he becomes an orthopedic surgeon and makes $400,000 per year, he can comfortably pay off his student loans and support a family.

However, the same medical student with $200,000 in debt who becomes a pediatrician and only makes $100,000 per year is in a far different situation. He may have a deep sense of satisfaction because he helps children, but you will have to live very frugally to pay off his loans. Otherwise, he will have to work so much that he gets burned out, develops an alcohol problem, and then has an affair with his nurse. Either way, your marriage is in serious trouble.

My final rule of thumb about knowing if a man ate the marshmallow or not is to ask yourself if you would go into business with him. If you don't trust him enough to go into business with him, why would you marry him?

In Review

- The ability to delay gratification is perhaps the most important psychological skill for both life and marriage.

- Your credit scores are a good measure of the ability to delay gratification and can predict future financial difficulties.
- A healthy lifestyle and staying fit also correlate with the ability to delay gratification and reduce the risk of early death and disability in men.
- Dedication to education and career are also signs of the ability to delay gratification and predict how well a man can provide for his family.
- If you wouldn't go into business with a man, why are you marrying him?

CHAPTER FOUR

Bonding and Chemistry

*L*et's switch gears and talk about another important requirement for a successful marriage: emotional stability. Humans have something psychologists call the Attachment System that governs how we relate to each other. This attachment system is so pervasive that it controls almost all interactions with other people, and even affects the relationships we have with our pets.

The attachment system initially develops based on how we relate to our mothers (or whoever cared for us as infants) or, more accurately, how they related to us. What makes the Attachment System so powerful is the fact that the system is recycled and reused repeatedly throughout our lives with all of our relationships. The system causes us to relate to other people, from friends to spouses, according to a specific attachment style.

The other reason why the system is so powerful is because it controls how you relate to your own children, which then causes your children to have the same attachment style you have. This is why attachment styles tend to be passed from generation to generation, much like genes for height, intelligence, and appearance. The attachment styles are usually life-long and are passed on so consistently that you can predict a child's attachment style before they are born, based on the mother's attachment style.

That said, the attachment styles are not set in stone and there are two positive ways they can be changed. You can go to psychotherapy for several years or you can be in a long-term relationship with someone who has a more-secure attachment style than you have. Pulling someone up and repairing their attachment style is hard work that comes on top of the normal relationship challenges, so don't say I didn't warn you. We'll get back to all of that in a moment.

The Strange Situation

In 1969, Mary Ainsworth, a famous psychologist, developed a test called the Strange Situation to classify what attachment style a baby has with its mother or primary caregiver. She originally demonstrated three attachment styles; her former students later discovered a fourth style.

Together, these four styles describe the basic patterns for relating to others that most people follow all their lives.

The way the Strange Situation test works is by briefly separating a young child between the ages of one and three from their mother and then watching the reunion. Trained evaluators observe from behind a one-way mirror to determine the attachment style based on what happens.

The test begins when a mother brings the young child into the observation room, places the child on the floor by some toys, and sits down in a chair. On the other side of the room, across the toys from the mother, is another chair that is empty. The mother is pre-instructed to encourage the child to play with the toys. After a few minutes of play, a female unknown to the child walks in and sits in the empty chair.

The unknown female then attempts to engage the child in play. After a few minutes, the mother's phone rings and the researchers tell her to leave the room. While the mother is gone, the female stranger again tries to engage the child in play or to comfort the child if the child becomes upset when the mother leaves. The mother stays out of the room for up to five minutes, if the child can tolerate it, and then returns. The reunion of the mother with the child is observed, which completes the experiment.

Of the four attachment styles, one is considered healthy or optimal and is called a Secure Attachment. The next two styles are considered sub-optimal and are called Insecure–Ambivalent and Insecure–Avoidant.

The fourth style is, thankfully, less common because it is really bad and is called a Disorganized Attachment style.

A **Securely attached child** who is tested with a strange situation reacts in a predictable way. They will play with the toys of the floor with little to no encouragement, but when the strange female walks in, they move closer to the mother and refuse to interact with the strange female. When the mother gets up to leave, they get upset and try to follow her. They continue to stay upset while the mother is gone, refuse to go to the strange female, and will not allow her to comfort them. When the mother returns, the child goes toward the mother and calms down quickly once the mother picks them up. This is the ideal reaction to the Strange Situation test.

The **Insecure–Ambivalent child** reacts a little differently. They also won't go to the stranger and do get upset when the mother leaves, but when the mother returns, the child acts more upset than they appeared to be while the mother was gone. Then the child takes a long time to calm down. In fact, the child is so upset when the mother returns that the child often hits the mother, as if to say, "Don't ever leave me like that again."

The **Insecure–Avoidant child** also avoids the unknown female, but when the mother gets up to leave the room, they don't seem to be upset. In fact, the child continues to calmly play with the toys while refusing to interact with a stranger. They also keep playing with the toys when the mother returns, and may not even look up at the mother. The child seems strangely calm throughout the process, but if you put a heart rate monitor on the child, the heart rate shoots up, which shows how internally stressed the child despite not showing it on the outside.

The **Disorganized child** responds to the strange situation test in one of two different ways. The child will either allow the unknown female to engage them in play and doesn't seem to have any fear of her, despite her being a stranger. In extreme cases, the child may even actively seek out the stranger and avoid the mother. Alternatively, the child will avoid both the mother and the stranger and do "disorganized" things like rock back and forth or bang their head in the corner. The child can also seem as if they are in a daze and won't play with the toys. If they do, it is in odd, limited ways, like making things spin or throwing and breaking the toys. The mother also tends to either ignore the odd behavior or yells and attempts to harshly punish the child.

Attachment Styles and Marriage

Not surprisingly, people with secure attachment styles tend to form stable relationships, which seem a bit boring to the other attachment styles. They tend to be attracted to each other because they see the insecure and disorganized attachment styles as either overly dramatic (Ambivalent) and crazy (Disorganized) or too reserved (Avoidant). If they do marry someone with an insecure attachment style, they can heal the insecure partner over several years with their calm and consistent approach to the relationship.

The one exception is people with disorganized attachment styles. Disorganized types are often so emotionally damaged that they need years of professional help to be able to form stable attachments and functional relationships.

The Insecure–Ambivalent attachment style is typically created by a mother who is distracted and somewhat inattentive to the child and the child's needs. The child learns to "turn up the volume" to get the mother's attention. This dramatic behavior then carries over into adult relationships, where they become jealous and clingy, requiring strong statements and constant displays of love from their partner.

On the flip side, such individuals also tend to be very expressive with their love, as well as highly seductive and romantic. As a result, they are often quite good at starting relationships, but sustaining them is another story. Despite these tendencies, they are capable of having a successful relationship if they are with the right person. If they end up with someone who is securely attached, their attachment style will stabilize and, over time, convert to a secure attachment style. However, if they end up with someone with either insecure attachment style, things get more complicated.

In the case of the Insecure–Avoidant attachment style, the mother has trained the child not to get upset or express distress. As the child grows up, they continue to repress their distress and have trouble expressing their feelings and desires. Even though they feel anxious and clingy on the inside, they appear to be aloof and uncaring to others on the outside. Romantic partners often perceive them as being excessively distant and unloving.

However, when their romantic partner starts to leave them, they feel overwhelmed by the impending loss and often panic. They can feel so threatened that it jolts them out of being reserved and into large expressions of the true depth of their feelings. Once the crisis is over, though, they quickly return to being stoic and unexpressive until the cycle repeats itself.

The disorganized attachment style is produced either by severe abuse and neglect by the primary caregiver, or by being raised in an orphanage or a revolving series of foster homes with no primary caregiver to bond to. These children are severely emotionally damaged. Without intensive, long-term treatment, they tend to grow up to be extremely manipulative, violent, and suicidal as adults.

Like Marilyn Monroe, who was severely abused by her schizophrenic mother and grew up in a revolving door of foster homes and orphanages, they form tumultuous, chaotic relationships and often end up killing themselves one way or another. It often takes years of professional treatment and arduously working on yourself to overcome such early damage, but I know people who have done exactly that and have become some of the most kind and loving people on this planet. They were then able to have successful marriages.

Recognizing people with disorganized attachment styles is important because, while they are often gorgeous and talented (like Marilyn), they are also extremely dangerous before they recover. Just as with lions and tigers, you don't want to get in the cage with them unless you are well-trained and know what you're doing. That is what we do as mental health professionals, but just like the lion tamer, we never let our guard down while we are in the cage.

Here are the things to look for to help you spot a man with a disorganized attachment style so you can stay away. First, he doesn't have a normal relationship with his family, if he even has a family at all. He was often raised by people other than the parents, such as relatives or, worse, in foster care. If he was lucky enough to be adopted, it is almost always after two years of age — that is when the Disorganized attachment style becomes relatively fixed and has to be treated professionally.

If you are even able to obtain accurate information about his biological parents, they tend to have severe drug problems, criminal histories, and multiple failed relationships. Not surprisingly, he most likely doesn't have a stable, supportive relationship with his parents.

Similarly, his biological siblings also tend to have problems with drugs, crime, and failed relationships. However, you may find exceptions, especially if the sibling was adopted before age two or managed to grow up with the same foster family the entire time. However, he still won't have a stable relationship with the resilient sibling due to his own disorganized attachment style.

Watch out for histories of frequent job changes and constantly moving from city to city. Men with disorganized attachment styles often resort to conning and manipulating others to survive, rather than supporting themselves honestly. As a result, they tend to move and change jobs frequently so people never get to know them well enough to see through their deception.

Their own histories of drug problems and criminal behavior are another big clue. They also tend to leave broken people and relationships in their wake like a tornado. Finally, they are not going to openly reveal these things to you. You will have to do your own research and possibly a background check to learn the details, but a lack of long-term, stable, loving relationships with their families is probably the easiest clue to spot.

What Attachment Style Do You Have?

Before you start cyber-stalking your friends and family to guess their attachment styles, you need to get a sense of your own so you know what to look for in a man. Take a few minutes to complete this non-scientific attachment survey. Give yourself one point for every question you can answer yes to, plus any bonuses:

1. Are your parents divorced or separated?
2. Did they divorce or separate before you turned 15 years old?
3. Did they divorce or separate before you turned 10 years old?
4. Did they divorce or separate before you turned 5 years old
5. Did they divorce or separate before you were a year old or were they never really together?

6. Were you raised by someone other than your biological mother? Give yourself one point for every different relative, foster home, and caregiver you lived with before you were 18 years old.

7. Was your mom or the main person who raised you: depressed, angry, gorgeous, a workaholic, alcoholic, a drug addict, or someone who went to prison?

8. Was your family overly proper and focused more on public appearances than on being close and having fun?

9. Did your mom (or primary care giver) have more than one husband/wife or live-in boyfriend/girlfriend? Give yourself one point for each person you grew up with who wasn't your biological father.

10. Did you move to different cities or neighborhoods, where you had to change schools during the school year? Give yourself one point for each move.

11. When was the last time you spoke with your mother or a supportive relative/foster parent? Give yourself one point if it has been more than a month, 2 points if it has been over six months, and 3 points if it has been over a year.

12. Give yourself a point for every time you have snooped through a boyfriend/husband's cellphone, e-mail, or apartment in the last year.

13. Do you hug your parents (or whoever raised you) if you haven't seen them in awhile? Give yourself 2 points if you haven't hugged them since you were a child and 5 points if you have no memory of ever being hugged by anyone who raised you.

14. Give yourself a point for every time you have cheated on a boyfriend/husband in your life.

15. Give yourself a point for every time you have forgiven a man and stayed with him after he cheated on you or hit you. (If the same guy cheated or hit you five times, that's 5 points.)

16. Give yourself a point for every time you have attacked or threatened to kill a boyfriend or husband.

17. Give yourself a point for every person you have had sex with on the day you met them.

18. Give yourself a point for every casual sexual relationship you have ever had.
19. Give yourself a point for every time someone has broken up with you because you were clingy, jealous, or crazy, or if they just disappeared on you without a word.
20. Do people tell you that you should be an actress? Give yourself 2 points if you actually became an actress.

Now add up all your points, including all the points from questions that ask if something happened multiple times. This isn't some kind of moral judgment or purity test. It is just a survey to estimate whether you have a secure or insecure attachment style. Plus, most of these things probably happened when you were a child and are not your fault. You survived it, so chin up.

Analyzing Your Results

0 to 5 Points = Secure Attachment: Wow, you are kind of boring, but that's good because it means you are securely attached. It also means you don't have to be super-careful about whom you marry. You can even marry someone who has an insecure style and be the loving, secure base to allow him to heal and become securely attached.

Just know that such a relationship will take extra work on top of the normal work of maintaining a marriage for at least several years. The best news is that you will be naturally attracted to securely attached men because you see the other attachment styles as a little crazy and won't have much chemistry with them.

6 to 10 Points = (Mostly) Secure Attachment: Not too bad, but you are in the gray zone between secure and insecure. What this means is that you are more likely to get pulled down if you end up with a guy who is less securely attached than you, so you need to limit yourself to securely attached men or you can get dragged down into some serious relationship drama that would take a lot of marriage counseling to fix, if it can be fixed at all.

The secret to marrying a securely attached guy is to watch out for the extremes and use your head to balance your heart. If you lean to the Avoidant (reserved) side, you will naturally be drawn to the intense chemistry of the romantic and expressive Ambivalent man. Instead, consciously choose to go for the loving and calm man with less chemistry who shows all the signs of secure attachment: a stable life with close and supportive relationships with his parents, siblings, and friends.

Similarly, if you lean to the Ambivalent (dramatic) side, you will be drawn to the strong and calm Avoidant male, who in turn will be powerfully drawn to your expressive and vivacious nature. Instead, consciously choose the more expressive and emotionally available man, provided he shows all the signs of being securely attached.

The trick is to go for the man who generates some, but not too much, chemistry. Intense chemistry is almost always a sign that both of you have significant attachment issues that will explosively trigger each other. In marriage, you want a smoothly functioning chemical plant and not a nuclear bomb that keeps going off.

10 to 20 Points = Insecure Attachment: You are solidly in one of the two insecure attachment styles. Your challenge is that you will be most strongly attracted to men who also have insecure styles, while securely attached men will seem a bit dull and boring. You will also be particularly vulnerable to the manipulations of men with disorganized attachment styles, so you have to be extra careful. You might be tempted to think that being with an insecure man isn't a bad thing because he will either balance you out or be like you and understand you better, but that is not what actually happens.

If you are on the Ambivalent (dramatic) side, your vivacious and spontaneous nature will tend to attract the strong and stable (more accurately, emotionally unavailable and non-expressive) male with an Avoidant style. Your relationship will work for a while, but eventually his silence and lack of expressiveness will frustrate you and make you feel like he doesn't love you or care about your feelings. Then you will either get in his face to provoke a reaction or try to leave, both of which will shock him into being more expressive for a while, but he'll eventually go back to his previously reserved and non-expressive style until the cycle repeats itself.

However, if you go for the romantic and expressive Ambivalent guy who understands how you feel, you will be literally playing with fire. At first, you will think you won the lottery because you are with a guy who knows how to satisfy your need for dramatic and over-the-top expressions of love. However, he needs the same thing, so what happens when you both need the same thing at the same time?

Inevitably, you will start competing with each other to get your needs met first and met more fully. As I said, when things are good, this guy is amazing in these kinds of relationships, but when things turn bad, you two will have explosive fights with dramatic breakups and passionate reunions. These relationships are never boring, but eventually the roller-coaster leaves you broken and exhausted.

Similarly, if you are on the Avoidant side, you will be the strong and stable one (i.e., emotionally unavailable and non-expressive) who is captivated by the spontaneity and passion for life of the Ambivalent guy. You and your dramatic man will have the same dysfunctional cycle, just with the roles reversed.

Relationships between two Avoidant people don't work well either, because both still need expressions of love and emotional sharing from each other, but neither can do it, so they have long periods of tense silence broken only by explosive arguments.

The obvious solution here is to marry a securely attached guy, but doing so is harder than it seems. When you meet a securely attached guy, it will seem like you only have a modest amount of chemistry. However, that is just your intensity-seeking, insecure attachment system talking. To pull this off and actually marry a securely attached guy, you will have to resist your craving for intensity and instead make your choice with your head and not your heart.

As I said, this isn't easy, but it is doable if you commit to marrying a good man who loves you rather than chasing after the guy who makes you feel the most loved. I will say it again: You must go for the guy who shows he loves you with a calm, consistent love rather than the guy who generates the most chemistry and makes you feel the most loved (by tapping into your insecure attachment style).

However, instead of trying to use your head to get it right, you can start long-term psychodynamic therapy (not cognitive behavioral therapy, also know as CBT) with a therapist who seems to get you and makes you feel comfortable. The good news is that you don't have to do 10 years of therapy before you can start dating. You only need a year or so if you keep going to therapy while you're dating. Your therapist can also help you make a good choice about whom to date and then can support you during the early years of your relationship, when your attachment issues inevitably get triggered. Check out Appendix II for tips on finding a psychotherapist.

20 to 30 Points = Deeply Insecure Attachment: "Houston, we have a problem." I'm sorry to say that you probably won't be able to just use your head to make a good choice and will need to go to psychotherapy for a while before you will be able to have a successful marriage or raise psychologically healthy children. I'm not saying you have a Disorganized attachment style; just that your attachment style is sufficiently insecure that you can't override it with logic. Yes, you could always luck out and end up with a securely attached guy, but the odds are not in your favor.

I know I am asking you to take a leap of faith and trust me, but think back over your life and your relationships. Have any of them been that successful? How many times did you seem to be with the perfect guy, only to have it blow up in your face, leaving you to wonder how you missed his obvious flaws? How many times have you met nice men who treat you really well, only to have them suddenly disappear on you with no explanation? How many times has your insecurity and fear of abandonment ruined a good relationship and driven away a kind and loving man?

I know how hard it is to accept that we are the cause of our relationship problems, because I was in your situation not that long ago. I had the same blind spots that caused me to miss obvious problems in other people. I would leave good women because they seemed a little dull or for something minor like an outfit they wore. Other times, my insecurity and fear of abandonment would make me so clingy that it drove them away.

I had an Insecure-Avoidant attachment style for most of my life, thanks to being in an adoption agency's nursery for several months as an infant and then being adopted by a reserved, unexpressive couple. As a young psychiatrist, I arrogantly believed that I didn't have an attachment problem since I didn't have suicidal thoughts or cut myself like my patients did. In fact, I only went to therapy in the first place because my girlfriend (who would later become my second wife) threatened break up with me if I didn't. When we were first dating, the consistent closeness of our relationship triggered me unconsciously to act out and create conflict and distance between us. I would break up with her and go back to dating a former girlfriend, then break up with the former girlfriend and get back together with my future wife, over and over again.

With the help of my therapist, I was able to stop the vicious cycle and eventually marry my second wife. Unfortunately, our marriage wasn't viable for other reasons despite the years of psychotherapy, deeply loving each other, and three excellent marriage therapists.

On the positive side, your therapy probably won't take as long as mine, because you will go into it accepting that you have attachment issues, and you won't be desperately trying to hold onto a marriage that was never viable. It may only take a year or so to make sufficient progress with your attachment style so you are able to make the positive choice of being with a man with a secure attachment and not fall for the intense chemistry of a man with an insecure or Disorganized style.

However, you will still need to continue seeing your therapist, because being in a relationship will powerfully trigger your attachment issues, even if you are with a securely attached man. The key is to pick a therapist you feel comfortable with and who seems to get you. Whether they have a PhD or just a master's degree isn't important, as long as they are comfortable doing psychodynamic psychotherapy. You don't want to go to someone who exclusively does cognitive behavioral therapy (CBT), which is excellent for anxiety and depression, but doesn't do much for attachment.

While you are in therapy, you will have to resist the urge to quit for a variety of reasons before you are done. Unlike CBT, psychodynamic psychotherapy often feels unstructured, and it can seem as if you aren't making progress. That is because it works at a deeper, unconscious level rather than on the superficial level of the conscious mind. It is also non-linear, meaning there are no specific steps in it as in CBT. It is more like slowly peeling an onion, one layer at time.

The key is to be patient and embrace the process. You may not feel any different at first, but over time, you will notice that you react differently from how you have in the past when faced with similar situations. Situations that would have overwhelmed you before will only moderately stress you and you will still be able to effectively deal with them.

Over 30 Points = Possible Disorganized Attachment: I don't want you to feel like I've given you a death sentence here. I'm just saying you might have a Disorganized attachment style. Obviously, I would have to evaluate you in person to be sure, but I think it is safe to say you struggle in relationships and would be better served by going to psychotherapy and focusing on healing your attachment issues than dating.

As I said earlier, I know people who have had Disorganized attachment styles from horrific abuse and neglect as children who have gone on to have healthy, loving marriages despite the odds. What they all had in common was that they accepted that their relationship problems were their fault and not someone else's. They avoided turning to drugs, alcohol, or other addictive behaviors to cope with their emotional pain and suffering. They also went to therapy at least once a week for years, which enabled them to choose to be with a loving and stable partner.

I would just recommend that you start a specialized type of psychotherapy called Dialectical Behavioral Therapy (DBT) first before trying to go to psychodynamic psychotherapy. DBT is specifically designed to treat the self-destructive behaviors and impulses caused by a Disorganized attachment style that make it difficult to benefit from other forms of psychotherapy. It typically takes one to two years of DBT to get the self-destructive behaviors under control so you can then start working directly on healing your attachment issue in psychodynamic psychotherapy.

Then plan on spending at least a couple of years in psychodynamic psychotherapy before dating. Your therapist can help you know when you are ready to start dating, but please realize that all this hard work has only moved you into the insecure attachment range and you will need to look exclusively for securely attached men to date and later marry.

What's *His* Attachment Style?

Now that you know your attachment style, let's take a look at his, because you will need to be able to tell something about it to know if he is a good fit for you.

Securely Attached (and Mostly Securely Attached) Men

Remember that, ideally, you will seek out a man with a secure attachment style regardless of your own attachment style. The securely attached man tends to do best in terms of being successful both professionally and personally. Such men have stable jobs and careers, and are comfortable in relationships as well. They tend to make good choices in terms of whom to marry and to avoid drama in their relationships. They lead quiet, happy lives with their families that may seem a little boring from the outside.

Insecure – Ambivalent Men

Insecure men are a little different. While they can do well in terms of job and careers, they often struggle with relationships. They tend to be anxious about their connection to you and can worry excessively about whether or not you love them. They need frequent reassurance and displays of love and commitment from you as well. Finally, they are also prone to jealousy and may struggle with fears of abandonment.

The difference between the two types of insecurely attached men — Ambivalent versus Avoidant — is how they express their anxiety within your relationship. Ambivalent guys are loud and "get up in your grille" with their anger and jealousy. They probably won't tell you why they are angry — men often express their negative emotions such as fear, sadness, grief, and worry as anger — or admit that they are actually scared of losing you or you leaving. However, if you look at the pattern of their anger and what triggers it, you will see that they are trying to possess you and keep you constantly focused on them.

Insecure – Avoidant Men

Avoidant guys are the exact opposite of Ambivalent guys — they are subtle and usually try to hide their anxiety about losing you, but you will sense the tension and their behavior will give it away. They tend to want to spend all their time with you and, when they are not with you, they are constantly texting or calling you on the phone. They may even stop hanging out with friends and family or their job may suffer because they spend so much time focused on you.

Most of the time, they will try to sweetly manipulate you into spending less time away from them with gifts and such. However, when that doesn't work or if they feel that you are ignoring them, their anger will surface, often in an explosive rage. Afterward, they will apologize sincerely, but the intensity of their rage may leave you shaken and a bit scared.

Disorganized Men

In contrast to the two insecure types of guys, the Disorganized guy is so severely affected by the attachment disruption that his entire life is affected, interfering with his education, career, and friendships, not just his romantic relationships. Such men tend to go to extremes, where they fall in love with you immediately and totally, but their love has no depth and they can cut you off just as quickly for trivial or even imagined reasons.

In fact, such men repetitively fall hard for women, convinced that they have found their soulmate after only a few dates (or a first date). A few weeks or months later, they will suddenly cut you off, convinced that you are a con artist or were cheating on them. Such a man also makes his ex sound like the most awful person in the world, even though he thought she was a saint and walked on water when he first met her. If you were a fly on the wall, you would have seen that his ex was never as amazing as he thought and then that he over-reacted to a minor misunderstanding or disagreement.

The Separation Test

Perhaps the easiest way to identify a guy's attachment style is by looking at how he handles physical separation. The secure guy easily tolerates being apart for a few days without difficulty. He may shoot you a text or leave a voice-mail to tell you he loves you, but it's no big deal if you don't respond. Afterward, when you do see each other, you will easily move back together, almost as if you hadn't been apart.

While the secure guy missed you, he was busy with other things like catching up with friends and getting projects done. He is glad to see you when you return, but he also appreciated having some time alone. This is the healthy pattern of a secure relationship, with an easy flow, back and forth — together, apart, and back together — like the ebb and flow of the tides or the gentle inhale and exhale of breathing during meditation.

The Ambivalent guy (Mr. Dramatic) is a little different. First, he may resist the idea of a few days' separation. If he is unable to prevent the separation, he may try to negotiate it down to as short of a time as possible or insist on a fixed schedule of contact such as every night. He will also get upset if the scheduled contact doesn't happen as planned, even if you have a good reason for missing it.

Alternatively, he may try to hide his anxiety and say he's fine with being a part for a few days, but then call and text you frequently. His jealousy will come out in the form of asking lots of questions about who you were with and what you are doing. He will be especially suspicious about any interactions with other men. Finally, he won't relax and calm down without an overt display of your commitment to him.

Another clue is that he will make you feel like you did something wrong while you were apart by not contacting him enough or for just talking to another guy, even if it was the plumber who was fixing your sink. He will often break the separation by "dropping by" for some dubious reason or find some excuse to be wherever you are going with your friends or family. It can be so creepy that if he weren't your boyfriend, you'd swear he was stalking you.

The Avoidant guy (Mr. Aloof) has similar anxiety and fears, but he expresses them differently. Instead of protesting the separation and seeking extra contact, he will act like he's fine and the separation is no big deal, but while you are apart, he's unconsciously convincing himself that you don't really love him and the relationship is over. When you do meet again, it's as if you are just friends and he has moved on. You will have to show him some overt sign that you still love him and that you are still in a relationship together before he will relax and open up. Of course, he will be excited, but you will get the sense that he was afraid (or secretly expected) things were over.

I once dated someone who really struggled with this. If we spent more than three days apart, she would become convinced that the relationship was over and I didn't love her. I could not change her mind over the phone, only in person. Nothing I could say was sufficient; only my physical presence could calm her. More than once, I found myself driving across town to her house late at night because she was convinced I didn't love her and that we were over. Even though our relationship was otherwise great, ultimately her fears doomed us.

A Disorganized guy reacts even more extremely to the separation test. He may forbid you from going or demand that he go along. He may also break up with you on the spot if you insist on going (which you should). Alternatively, he may follow you and blatantly stalk you the entire time. If he somehow manages not to do any of these things, he will probably get stinking drunk or high the whole time you are gone. He may even cheat on you and afterward insist that you were the one who wanted to take a break so he did nothing wrong. Of course, his ultimate reaction is to accuse you of cheating during your trip; even if you somehow persuade him otherwise, he will still make you feel guilty for going.

In Review

- There are four attachment styles that govern our relationships throughout our lives, from romantic relationships to friendships to parenting.

- The secure attachment style produces the most stable relationships and can even help heal insecure attachment styles in others over time.
- There are two anxious, insecure attachment styles, Ambivalent and Avoidant, that can still form successful relationships and marriages if they are with securely attached partners.
- The Ambivalent attachment style tends to be dramatic and is most strongly attracted to the Avoidant style, but actually does the best with a securely attached partner.
- The Avoidant style is reserved and unexpressive, and most strongly attracted to the Ambivalent style, but actually does the best with a securely attached partner.
- The Disorganized attachment style is associated with major life disruption and often requires years of therapy before being able to have successful relationships.

STEP III

The Relationship Archetypes

CHAPTER FIVE

The Spectrums

$\mathcal{B}$efore I explain what the spectrums are, I want you to take these two surveys. I am intentionally not telling you what the surveys or the spectrums are about because I want to limit any bias and obtain as accurate an assessment as possible about where you score on the two spectrums.

With no further ado, pull out a pen and some paper to keep score. Record how many times you select answer A and how many times you answer B for each quiz. There are no right or wrong answers here — just go with your initial impression and don't think too much about your answer or why I'm asking the question. Answer every question even if your answer is only slightly true about you.

Survey 1

1) If you got a modest inheritance unexpectedly and you needed to figure out what to do with the money (assuming you didn't know much about finance or investing), would you:

   A. Turn the money over to a reputable financial advisor to manage it for you?
   B. Teach yourself all about investing so you can invest it yourself?

2) If you are meeting a friend for dinner, do you prefer to:

   A. Go along with the restaurant your friend suggests?
   B. Pick the restaurant yourself so you know you will both enjoy dinner?

3) If you have an important decision to make, do you tend to:

   A. Follow the advice of experts?
   B. Trust your own opinions and logic?

4) If you and your friends were throwing a surprise birthday party for another friend, would you be more likely to:

   A. Bring your famous meatballs?
   B. Host the party so everyone would have a great time?

5) In bed, do you prefer:

   A. Being deliciously taken?
   B. Being in charge and blowing his mind?

6) Would your friends be more likely describe you as being:

   A. A good listener?
   B. A good problem solver?

7) When it comes to important decisions in your personal life, are you more likely to:

   A. Take your time thinking about it and doing plenty of research?
   B. Make your decision quickly with a minimal amount of research?

8) If you were going on a road trip with a friend, would you prefer to be:

A. The passenger?
B. The driver?

9) When it comes to making tough decisions, do you prefer to:

A. Trust someone smarter and more experienced to make the decision?
B. Take personal responsibility for the decision, right or wrong?

10) When it comes to dating, are you more likely to:

A. drop hints?
B. invite him on the fabulous date you've planned?

11) If it was your birthday, would you prefer:

A. For your friends to throw you a surprise birthday party?
B. Throwing an awesome party yourself that your friends keep raving over?

Save your answers because we'll score them later. Now take the second survey. Record your answers the same way — by keeping track of the number of times you answer A versus B. Keep your answers for this survey separate from first survey, because we will score them separately.

Survey 2

1. When it comes to money in a relationship:

A. You prefer that he makes more than you do, even if you make plenty.
B. You don't really care who makes more.

2. If you were to start a family with your future husband, would you prefer:

   A. To stay home with your child for a few years while he or she is young?
   B. To go back to work immediately and let him stay home with your child?

3. When it comes to financial responsibilities in a marriage, do you prefer to:

   A. Use your paycheck for the "extras" such as entertainment, vacations, and other luxuries?
   B. Be responsible for the staples, such as the mortgage, bills, and retirement savings?

4. When it comes to having your own children, do you see them as more of a:

   A. Blessing?
   B. Responsibility?

5. If you were going to pick up a new hobby, would you be more likely to:

   A. Take up yoga?
   B. Train in a martial art?

6. If you are going out on the town on a date and you want to look your best (and he is a lot taller than you), would the heels on your shoes be:

   A. Over 3 inches?
   B. Under 3 inches?

7. During sex, would you prefer to:

    A. Be tied up and spanked?
    B. Tie him up and do the spanking?

8. When it comes to makeup, do you prefer to:

    A. Look your best?
    B. Keep it light and subtle?

9. Would you be more likely to move across the country for your:

    A. Relationship?
    B. Career?

10. If you were going clubbing on a Saturday night with your friends, would you be more likely to wear:

    A. A dress?
    B. Pants?

11. If you were playing a game with a dear friend that was a bit down, would you be more likely to:

    A. Not play as hard and maybe let them win?
    B. Try to beat the stuffing out of them?

Scoring

Add up every A and B from the first quiz and see which you have more of. Next, add up all every A and B from the second quiz and see if you have more of A or of B.

The Leader/Supporter Spectrum

The purpose of the first quiz is to determine where you fall on the Leader/ Supporter Spectrum. While I've used the terms leader and supporter, another way to think about it might be as the Initiator/Facilitator Spectrum.

Leadership is often mistakenly associated with domination and control, but it is actually about vision and inspiration. Similarly, being a supporter is mistakenly associated with being passive or powerless rather than as an essential partner in fulfilling a vision.

The reality is that neither leading nor supporting are superior or more valuable than the other; they are merely different. In ballroom dancing, is one dancer better than the other simply because one is leading and the other following? Was Fred Astaire a better dancer than Ginger Rogers? After all, Ginger did do everything Fred did — only backward and in high heels. If anything, both dancers have to perform their different roles well to produce the elegant synergy of ballroom dancing.

To take the ballroom dancing analogy further, the goal of the leader is not to draw attention to themselves or to control, but rather to highlight the beauty and elegance of their partner. Similarly, in marriage, the true job of the leader is not to dominate or have their way, but rather to lead their partner to greater joy and pleasure. Furthermore, supporters are far from powerless in a marriage. They exert their power not through planning or initiating, but by exercising veto power over plans and decisions.

Yes, the supporter always has the power and right to veto any and all of the plans and ideas of the leader. For example, the leader may suggest a certain restaurant for dinner, but the supporter may not be feeling it and will say something like, "No, we ate there last week, plus the food is a little heavy and I'm in the mood for something lighter." The leader then can respond with a different suggestion; someplace with lighter fare that they haven't been to in awhile.

Ideally, this explanation will help you set aside any biases about one being better or superior to the other. I also want to be clear that the Leader/ Supporter Spectrum only applies to your personal life and not your career. You could be the CEO of a Fortune 500 company at work, but when you get home, you prefer to relax into your true nature as a supporter.

Alternatively, you may get bossed around all day a work and can't wait to get home to satisfy your need to lead.

Playing the Role (Sometimes)

Another misconception regarding leading and supporting in relationships is assuming that the roles are rigidly fixed and the leader always leads while the supporter always follows. A better way to think about it is to look at the number of areas where one person needs to lead.

A stronger leader might lead in eight out of 10 areas, but then play the supportive role in the other two areas. A more moderate leader might only lead in six out of 10 areas and be supportive in the remaining four areas. For example, one partner may lead when it comes to finances, but then is supportive when it comes to decorating. The roles may also differ in a single area, such as vacations, where one partner may plan trips to visit family while the other plans the romantic getaways.

My point is that being a leader or supporter means only that you tend to play that role a bit more than the other, not that you always play the same role. What typically determines who leads and who supports for a specific area or issue is how strongly each partner feels about the area and whether they have a clear vision regarding what to do with it. Even the strongest supporter will often have an area or two they care deeply about, along with a grand vision for that area of your life. That is precisely when even the strongest leader wisely shifts into the supportive role. At least, that is how it is supposed to work.

The Two Gunfighters (AKA Two Leaders)

When two leaders are in a relationship together, their natural leadership energies tend to clash, especially when they both care deeply about something, but have different visions. Similar to the old western movies where the two gunfighters would look at each other and say, "This town isn't big enough for the both of us," leaders struggle to co-exist with each other in the confined space of a marriage. While it is possible to resolve conflicting visions, constantly having to negotiate and compromise on every little issue that comes up is exhausting.

When I first met my second wife, I had recently graduated from medical school and was just starting my training in psychiatry. She had already finished her medical training and was working as a physician in the community. Like many physicians, she is a strong leader. In fact, her strength and skill as a leader was one of the things that attracted me to her.

While I have always been a strong leader, being a new doctor fresh out of medical school makes you feel incompetent on a daily basis. In addition, working 100+ hours a week saps all of your time and energy, so in the beginning, I was happy to let her do all the leading. However, as I advanced in my training as a psychiatrist and began having more time and energy, my own natural leadership style re-emerged and I started chafing under her leadership more and more.

It was not that I disagreed with her vision for our life and marriage together so much as I just wanted to work on my own projects and goals as well. We still loved each other very much and tried everything to save our marriage. We even spent over a year each with three different marriage counselors. Despite our enormous efforts to save our marriage, though, we were never able to solve the inherent conflict caused by both of us being strong leaders in too many of the same areas of our life together.

The Dirty Dishes Problem (AKA Two Supporters)

Similarly, couples struggle when both are supporters and reluctant to take the leadership role. This is most problematic when neither one cares about an important issue and allows the situation to languish until it becomes a crisis that can no longer be ignored. Even if one person eventually steps up to solve the crisis, there are still negative consequences for the relationship.

This is the "dirty dishes problem." If no one takes responsibility for keeping the kitchen clean, the dirty dishes build up until someone's dirt tolerance is exceeded and that person washes them because they can't stand it anymore. While the dishes get washed, the person doing the washing often resents their partner for making them do it. As the pattern continues, even something as minor as dirty dishes can do serious damage to a relationship.

It was that way with my wife's previous marriage. She would often end up leading because things were not getting done and she couldn't stand it anymore. While she was good at leading, she didn't enjoy it. Constantly being forced into being the leader eventually built up enough resentment in my wife that it was a significant factor in ending her 13-year marriage despite their having been happy with each other for many years.

Interpreting Quiz 1 – Your Leader/Supporter Nature

A > B – You're a Supporter: While you may be a leader at work, you don't want to have to lead at home. You don't mind him driving — or taking the lead in bed — most of the time. You also love it when he surprises you. However, you do have a few areas that you assert yourself in, which could be anything from your monthly budget to the decorating. One clue that can help confirm that you are more of a supporter than a leader is if you are more comfortable giving appreciation than receiving it.

Your challenge is to choose a man who is a strong enough leader that he doesn't frustrate you with his passivity, yet isn't so strong that you start feeling controlled. One way to tell if he is too strong a leader is if he makes too many of the decisions alone or if he ignores your request to lead in the areas you care strongly about. Pay attention if it feels as if he doesn't listen to you, because that could be a sign that he is too strong a leader for you.

Similarly, you need to avoid going for a man who isn't enough of a leader (or is actually a supporter). You can tell if a man isn't enough of a leader if he seems a little lazy and that things don't get done if you don't step up and make it happen. Another sign that he is not enough of a leader is if he tries too hard to please you. His mantra is "whatever you want," which at first may seem sweet and loving, but over time, you will come see that he is just throwing the monkey onto your back.

Initially, some men seem strong enough, but they may be pushing themselves to appear as if they are a stronger leader than they actually are. Watch for signs that he finds leading to be more of a burden than a joy. We can all push ourselves to take on an unnatural role for a while, but no one can fake it long-term. Over time, working outside our nature takes effort and uses up valuable emotional and mental energy, which leads to exhaustion, frustration, and the relationship killer: resentment.

Similarly, you also need to make sure he is the right kind of leader. Not every leader leads for the right reason. You will know a true leader because his greatest joy comes from leading you to your greatest pleasure. On the other hand, the false leader leads because he is selfish or is too afraid to trust others, and the worst leaders lead because they enjoy dominating and abusing others. Watch carefully to see what motivates him to lead so you can tell the noble king from the petty tyrant.

B > A - You're a Leader: You enjoy leading most of the time at home, although not all of the time. While you are passionate about many things, there are other things you just don't care much about. Maybe your career or other projects take up so much of your time and energy that you appreciate it when someone else takes over the social calendar or running your home. As a result, you can easily slip into the role of being a great supporter when the situation calls for it.

Your perfect man will not feel strongly about many areas of your life together and is comfortable letting you lead in those areas. However, he will feel strongly about a few areas that could be anything from your vacations to how the children are raised. Not surprisingly, he will prefer to lead in those areas.

The trick is finding that balance — someone who doesn't want to lead so much that it causes power struggles, or so little that you are frustrated and stressed with more responsibilities than you want. That way, you won't have so many areas you both feel strongly about that you'll have to negotiate and compromise over.

However, if you are large and in charge and making it happen, your challenge isn't just to find a good supporter who rarely needs to lead. You also need to learn to appreciate all the little things he does to help you stay calm and not get too frustrated.

As a good supporter, he will help you work out the details and do the mundane tasks required for your plans to succeed. You also have to be careful to not slip into domination or into being selfish and trying to get your way all the time. Being selfish is a constant risk because your supporter partner isn't going to stop you (until they are so upset they are ready to file for divorce). You must monitor yourself and be disciplined. Always remember to lead your partner to their joy and delight. Your greatest pleasure should be their smile.

The Masculine–Feminine Spectrum

The purpose of the second quiz was to determine where you fall on the Masculine-Feminine Spectrum. You probably noticed from the questions that I'm using fairly traditional definitions of masculine and feminine, with protecting and providing associated with the masculine and nurturing, relating, and creativity with the feminine.

I'm not doing this to perpetuate old stereotypes, but rather to accurately describe your true nature. Thanks to decades of psychological research on gender, we now know that most of us are complex blends with varying degrees of masculine and feminine traits that don't always correspond to our plumbing.

For clarity, here is a list of personality traits and how I am classifying them in my system. I'm not saying this is the best or most accurate way to classify these personality traits; merely that for the purpose of the system, this is how they have to be classified.

Masculine Traits:

- Naturally seeks to physically protect loved ones.
- Enjoys providing for love ones financially.
- Enjoys competition and isn't significantly affected by the loser's feelings when they win.
- Tends to value logic over feelings or creativity.
- Fascinated by mechanical and technical things, and enjoys using and fixing them.
- Less sensitive to the feelings of others than average.
- Tends to value functionality over esthetics.
- Uncomfortable with babies and young children.
- Communicates through action better than with words.

Feminine Traits:

- Values relationships and naturally seeks to enhance and maintain them.
- Tends to value feelings and creativity over logic.

- Dislikes competition because of concern for the loser's feelings and values relationships over winning.
- Fascinated by people and relationships.
- Less interested in technical and mechanical things.
- Sensitive to the feelings of others.
- Tends to value esthetics and design over functionality.
- Naturally drawn to babies and young children.
- Communicates well verbally and enjoys conversation.

Again, I'm not trying perpetuate stereotypes here. I'm just establishing a basis for discussion and to simplify how to work with these complementary energies. Despite our ancestors' failure to appreciate our complexity, they did accurately recognize that masculine and feminine energies still naturally complement each other well, so there is no need to fix what isn't broken. The part we do need to fix is attaching masculine and feminine traits to specific genders.

The Superior Results of Synergy

If you look at the roles of masculine and feminine energy in relationships, you can see how both are valuable. Protecting and providing are important, as are nurturing and relationship building. All of these roles are important, but they are different enough that it would be a challenge for a single person to excel at all of them. It is much easier to collectively cover the roles with each partner specializing to a degree than for both of you to try to be excellent at all of them.

What actually works best is to balance the masculine and feminine energies in a relationship so they complement each other and can combine synergistically to produce something superior to the individual parts. If you think about it, having every role covered in a relationship is like having a complete set of tools in your toolbox to fix any problem that comes up. As our modern world becomes more and more complex, the challenges that relationships face grow right along with it.

The Spectrum Showdown

There are other reasons why balancing the masculine and feminine also works in relationships. Balanced masculine and feminine energies also produce sustained romantic and sexual attraction and compatibility in relationships.

For example, hot masculine men and women hook up all the time, thanks to their aggressive sexual tendencies, but it is usually just that — a hookup, not a lasting relationship. The urge to take things forward is rarely present or quickly fades. This is because masculine energy is competitive by nature and automatically seeks to dominate when it is in the presence of other masculine energy. What's more, this automatic competition is unconscious and almost impossible to resist.

Similarly, feminine-feminine combinations also struggle. They tend to get along well and be emotionally close, but we know from research that such relationships suffer sexually to the point that they are almost better classified as friendships rather than romantic relationships. After all, someone has to step up and make it happen in bed.

Using the Masculine-Feminine Spectrum

What can you do to avoid this masculine/feminine imbalance?

First, be aware that the blend of masculine and feminine energy you present at work is not necessarily the same as the blend in your personal life. That is because we tend to push ourselves to be successful in our careers even if it means developing and using traits and energies that are not natural to us. Masculine managers often have to learn to mimic feminine traits to better nurture, develop, and relate to their subordinates. Feminine managers often have to learn to be tough to hold their subordinates accountable and enforce rules and regulations.

Second, realize that the blend in your personal life is what is important when it comes to marriage. We can push ourselves to function outside our true natures during the time we spend at work, but once we get home, we rarely have the energy to be who we are not. Think about it — can you really act like someone you are not 24/7? I certainly can't.

Adhering as closely as possible to your true nature is key. After all, we only have so much energy on a daily basis. If we blow too much on faking it in our relationship, we aren't going to have much left for the rest of our day.

Third, if you know what your ratio of masculine to feminine energy is, you can seek out a man who balances and complements you. If you lean to the feminine side, you can partner with a male who is masculine enough to maintain romantic and sexual attraction, but not so masculine that you feel as if you are with a caveman.

Alternatively, if you are more masculine than feminine, a somewhat feminine man will not compete with you or try to dominate you. He will instead enhance your life with his gentleness and sensitivity to your feelings and needs. He might even stay home to raise your children while you get to lean into your career.

I have seen this masculine woman/feminine man pairing work extremely well over the years, thanks to my time as a young man in the military and being in the medical field. Both the military and medicine have a number of masculine women, and I have consistently noticed that their husbands were gentle and nurturing — you could see how their feminine energies complemented the masculine energies of their wives.

Interpreting Quiz 2 — Your Masculine/Feminine Nature

A > B – You Lean to the Feminine Side: Your feminine side is your dominant side and it expresses itself through your creativity and joy in helping and nurturing others. You also tend to approach people and situations from an emotional or values-based perspective, such as with kindness, fairness, and compassion. You also probably relate well to others, both male and female. That said, you can still shift into your masculine side to be tough and protective when necessary.

You also tend to be comfortable with children and babies. If you have a family together, you expect to play a major role in raising them. However, that doesn't mean you are willing to give up your career and stay home. Similarly, being feminine doesn't mean you automatically want children, because you can just as easily express your feminine side through your career by being in a helping profession or a creative field.

Another clue that confirms you lean to the feminine side is what kind of man you are attracted to. You are naturally attracted to men who are strong, confident, and protective instead of more sensitive ones. That is not to say you want a macho man. You just don't want a man who cries at the drop of a hat.

B > A – You Lean to the Masculine Side: You can put on a dress and wear makeup if the occasion calls for it, but jeans and sportswear are your staple. You also enjoy competition, but can turn it off with friends without feeling bored. You can hang and drink with the guys, but if one of your girls calls with an emotional problem, you'll be there. You approach people and situations logically and aren't easily swayed by a sob story.

You are also probably quite successful in your career, but your dating life may be another story. While sex is not an issue, you can handle a hookup if you decide to have one. Getting dates is tricky because you may feel like the flirting gene was removed from both of your X chromosomes and it's just easier for you to ask him out. However, when you start dating someone, it rarely turns into a relationship because men tend to disappear on you. You may not have realized why, but men sense that there is something different about you even if they can't explain it – they were sensing your masculine energy.

The solution to your relationship dilemma is to go for a guy who is somewhat more into his feminine side, because you will get along better with that somewhat feminine guy. He will be sensitive to your feelings and be comfortable expressing his as well. He also will add a creative spark to your relationship; that little something extra that was lacking in your past relationships with more masculine guys. He will also appreciate it if you dominate him from time to time, and not just in bed.

However, it is also important that you not try to dominate him too much. While he leans to the feminine, he still has a masculine side that needs to remain healthy for your relationship to work in the long term. You especially have to be careful not to emasculate him. Masculine energy doesn't just compete; it often seeks to dominate, and one way it does this is by weakening any masculine energy around it. You must avoid unconsciously emasculating your man or you will push him too far into his feminine side.

One form unconscious emasculation takes is by criticizing him for being a narcissist, arrogant, or too cocky. Being cocky is a form of confidence, not arrogance, and is a sign of a healthy masculinity, so praise his confidence.

Another form of unconscious emasculation is to restrict the space for his masculinity to the point that it withers and dies. Masculinity needs to express itself to be healthy. That means you will have to step out of your masculine side occasionally to let his take over. Don't expect his masculinity to be healthy and strong in the bedroom, if you never give it space to flourish in day-to-day life.

In Review

- Quiz 1 assessed where you fall on the Leader/Supporter Spectrum and determined whether you are a leader or supporter.
- Leaders and supporters complement each other naturally and work well together in relationships.
- Quiz 2 assessed where you fall on the Masculine/Feminine Spectrum and determined whether you lean to the masculine or feminine side.
- Masculine and feminine energies naturally attract and work well together in relationships.

CHAPTER SIX

Putting It Together

*N*ow that we have determined where you fall on Leader/Supporter and Masculine/Feminine Spectrums, let's put them together so we start using them to find your complement.

Start by combining your two classifications. You should end up with one of four possible combinations: Masculine Leader, Masculine Supporter, Feminine Leader or Feminine Supporter. Please only read the section for your combination, where I reveal your complementary archetype, the type of man you will have the best marriage with, along with his shadow archetype.

Shadow archetypes resemble complementary archetypes in almost every way, but are the opposite side of the same coin. Much like the Jedi knights in "Star Wars," men must choose to live in the light where they can be great husbands and fathers or succumb to the seductive power of the dark side and forever be a shadow of what they could be.

The problem is that the four primary male archetypes and their shadows resemble each other so closely that it is not easy to tell them apart. He may not even realize that he's been seduced by the dark side. But I will teach you how to easily spot each type of shadow from across the room (or within a few dates at most) in the chapters on each complementary archetype.

Again, please resist any urges to read about the other combinations because they were not written for you and you will risk getting confused and misapplying the system. If you strongly disagree with your classification, it is more likely that you are biased against the classification than that the classification is inaccurate.

Maybe you resent being called a supporter and find it insulting because it implies that you are somehow weak (which you are not). Maybe you cringe at the thought of being called masculine because you feel that it implies that you are some how secretly gay (which you are not, either). Instead, realize that no category is better than another and that we are, in fact, complex blends of all of these traits. No one is completely one thing without any trace of the others. We are just classifying which way you lean, not labeling you as a person.

Even if you continue to disagree with your classification, please still work through the rest of this book using that classification, to give the system a chance to work for you. After all, it is just a term to assist you in achieving your ultimate goal of marrying the man meant for you. Once that happens, you can ditch the label and never think about it again. Now skip to your section below...

Feminine Supporter

As a feminine supporter, the type of male you will do best with is a masculine leader. I am not talking about the type of marriage where the man is in charge and wife is submissive. That type of marriage just doesn't work any more (if it ever did). Rather, I am talking about a man who protects and provides for you while you enrich his life with your nurturance and creativity; a man who plans and initiates, but doesn't control you and respects your power to veto.

I am also only talking about your personal life here, not how you are at work. You may be CEO of a Fortune 500 company, but the question is what kind of marriage will bring you the most joy and satisfaction. If your marriage works well, you will have more energy, both physically and emotionally, to put into your high-powered career. Being a supporter at home does not mean you are a supporter everywhere else.

I am also not calling you weak. There's nothing weak about being feminine or a supporter. I'm from the South and I assure you there is nothing weak about southern belles, who are perhaps the best example of a true Feminine Supporter archetype. Go watch "Gone with the Wind" if you have any doubts about what I am saying.

I call your complementary Masculine/Leader archetype **The Athlete**. I don't literally mean he is an athlete (although he could be). What I mean is, like an athlete, he is highly competitive and doesn't shrink from conflict. In fact, he probably thrives on competition. For example, he may be a trial lawyer or work in a competitive field such as finance or sales. Alternatively, he may be in a hierarchical field such as surgery, the military, or law enforcement. The point is that he plays to win and takes responsibility for his decisions.

However, before you run off in search of your Rhett Butler, you must first learn how to spot his shadow, the **Godfather**. I will teach you how to spot a godfather from little more than a conversation, long before you are at risk of falling dangerously in love with someone who thinks he is above the rules or the law. To learn how to identify and attract your Athlete, go to Chapter 7.

Feminine Leader

As a feminine leader, you may love your dresses, heels, and makeup, but you also love being in charge. Just as you can't judge a book by its cover, people often underestimate you because they don't look past your pretty surface. I grew up in the South and a lot of southern belles are feminine leaders just like you.

While you are quite successful professionally, you can struggle when it comes to romance and relationships. Your relationships tend to start fabulously well, but then quickly descend into power struggles and screaming arguments. Even more puzzlingly, men disappear on you even when your relationship seems to be going well.

The problem is that while you are appropriately attracted to masculine guys, you mistakenly go for ones who are also leaders. As a result, your leadership energies clash instead of complementing each other. That is why you get into so many heated arguments in your relationships. It is also why men disappear on you. They may not be able to put their finger on what exactly is wrong, but they sense something is not right and just move on.

The solution to your dating woes is to shift your focus slightly from the masculine leader to the masculine supporter. You will still be attracted to his masculinity, but his preference to support won't clash with your need to lead. I call your complementary archetype the **Engineer.**

The Engineer is clearly masculine and tends to love technology and mechanical things, as well as being highly intelligent. His valuable technical skills often allow him to earn decent money. He is often more logical than emotional (sometimes to a fault), but that is why he will be powerfully attracted to your femininity, your expressiveness, and your values-based approach to life.

Before you set off in search of your Engineer, you need be beware his shadow, the Gamer. Gamers resemble Engineers in many ways, but their addiction to video games and technology make them poor husbands. Skip ahead to Chapter 8 to get started on finding your complement.

Masculine Supporter

As a masculine supporter, you are in the difficult situation where you don't tend to attract many guys, but you also don't feel comfortable approaching guys, so your dates are few and far between. The problem is that many guys are at least somewhat masculine, so they tend to be put off by your masculine energy. The problem is further compounded by the fact that most feminine guys also tend to be supporters, so, although they might be interested, they won't approach you first. You are probably frustrated by how many times you've caught a cute guy checking you out who never tries to bust a move.

What that means is that you are looking for a rare type of male; one who is both feminine and a leader. I call your complementary archetype the **Film Director** because he has to be strongly connected to his feminine side, since that is where his creativity comes from. Yet at the same time, he also has to be a strong leader to (metaphorically) organize and direct the film crew and actors to successfully produce something as complex as a film.

Before you start crashing movie sets looking for your Film Director, you also need to know how to differentiate him from his shadow archetype, the **Rock Star**. They are both feminine leaders, but the Rock Star has been seduced by the dark side and would rather party and sleep around than be the great husband he is capable of. Skip to Chapter 9 to learn how to catch your rare bird, while side-stepping his shadow.

Masculine Leader

As a Masculine Leader, you are large and in charge and making it happen ... until it comes to your relationships. You are comfortable approaching guys and taking them home, but the problem is that this only leads to a hookup or two and nothing that lasts. Your assertive masculine sexual energy creates plenty of sparks with masculine guys and the sex is amazing, but then they disappear on you. Even worse, they only show up for a booty call and get squirrelly if you even hint that you desire anything more.

You are probably scratching your head and wondering why this keeps happening. Being masculine and straightforward, you probably tracked a few down to demand an answer. If you somehow managed to get one to respond, he basically said that even though the sex was great, there just wasn't any chemistry, which left you thinking, "What the hell?"

What he is trying to tell you (masculine guys aren't very good at talking about their feelings) is that there is no emotional connection for building a relationship beyond the amazing sex. The deeper issue that he can't quite put his finger on is that your masculine energy repels his. In addition, if he is a masculine leader, your need to lead will repel him even more. Don't despair, though: You do have a complementary archetype that won't run and actually wants to be with you called the **Artist**.

Your Artist will be powerfully attracted to you, both emotionally and physically, but he won't approach you. Yes, you will have to learn how to identify and pursue him (I will teach you how), but first you need to learn how to distinguish your Artist from his lazy, irresponsible shadow, the **MAW** (Model/Actor/Whatever). Skip ahead to Chapter 10 to get started.

In Review

- Combine your two basic classifications on the two spectrums to identify which of the four categories you fit in: Feminine Supporter, Feminine Leader, Masculine Supporter, and Masculine Leader.
- Only read the section corresponding to your category, which will reveal your complementary archetype.
- Each complementary archetype has a shadow archetype that strongly resembles it, due to having the same energies, but isn't appropriate for marriage for reasons you will soon learn.

CHAPTER SEVEN

The Athlete

Your Athlete may not literally be a professional athlete, but he will be highly competitive, since all top athletes are and will play to win in most areas of his life. As a result, he may have a career in a competitive field such as being a trial lawyer, business executive, or commission-based salesman. He may even play for all the marbles as an entrepreneur with his own startup.

Alternatively, he may express his competitive nature through other ways, such as his choice of hobbies. He may be a serious amateur athlete or chess master, or someone who geeks out by restoring and showing cars. He will probably be a rabid sports fan as well (nobody's perfect). The point is that winning is important to him and he will seek out competition in at least one area of his life (but still know when to turn it off with friends and loved ones).

Another defining trait of your Athlete is that he is fiercely protective of the people he loves and will not shrink from conflict when danger arises. He may express his protective nature in his career choice by serving in the military or law enforcement, or volunteer on the side as a firefighter. His protective instincts will show up almost immediately — he will walk you to your car or hail you a taxi at the end of your first date. He will make you feel safe around him.

He will show other chivalrous behaviors as well, such opening doors, pull out chairs, and helping you put on your coat. Don't be offended by his old-fashioned ways; instead, see them as signs that he cares about you. Besides, a lack of such behaviors in a masculine leader is a red flag that he may be a Godfather, the shadow archetype of an Athlete, which we will discuss later in the next section.

Besides his career choice and protective nature, you will know an Athlete by his confidence. He will be calm and friendly when he approaches you rather than shy and hesitant. He may exude so much confidence that he walks the edge of being an arrogant jerk, but doesn't quite cross the line thanks to his sense of humor. He also has an unspoken edge. Even though he may be the friendliest guy at a party, you will have a sense that people don't want to be rude or disrespectful to him and risk making him angry.

Don't be surprised if your Athlete is more conservative than you are or that he is not a vegan or into yoga like you. He may even be more religious. That's not really a problem — you need your relational styles to be complementary more than you need your values to match perfectly. He shouldn't make too much fun of your interests or disrespect you for his own amusement, but don't expect him to be just like you or into everything you're into, either.

Let me give you an example of this principle of complementing relationally, rather than matching in terms of values or interests. I know a guy who is an accounting executive at a large company. He's also a Republican, a Christian, and an NRA member. He supports the death penalty, but he also has a heart of gold and would take a bullet to protect someone in danger.

His wife is a yoga teacher, a Democrat, and a Buddhist, and has lots of tattoos and piercings that he hates. He likes to do triathlons and hunt and fish. She would rather read a book or go to a meditation retreat. They are polar opposites in so many ways, but when you see them together, their chemistry is so electric you would never guess that they have been together for almost 15 years. They flow smoothly as a couple, with him leading in most areas while she solidly supports him.

The Ultimate Athlete

Here is a sample profile of an Athlete to help create an image in your mind's eye so you will know him when you see him:

- **Age**: 5 to 10 years older than you (but not more than 15 years older, and never younger than you)
- **Grooming**: short, neatly groomed hair, clean-shaven or neatly groomed facial hair
- **Height**: 4 to 8 inches taller than you (you want to be able to wear your best heels with him, don't you?)
- **Build**: muscular — you can tell he works out (no potbellies because they are a sign of poor health and predictor of an early death in males)
- **Clothing**: conservative, a dress shirt and jeans in a casual setting, a blue or gray suit at work or in a formal setting, athletic wear on the weekends because he's probably going to or coming from the gym
- **Accessories**: quality watch (think a diver's or sports watch), no piercings or flashy rings (not like Godfathers, who tend to like their bling), no visible tattoos when he's in a long-sleeved shirt
- **Hats**: unless he's a cowboy, only wears a baseball cap occasionally and only with the bill to the front, like a baseball player
- **Shoes**: conservative, well-polished dress shoes at work (cowboy boots are also acceptable in the south or western U.S.), worn tennis/running shoes otherwise.
- **Hobbies**: outdoor hobbies will include active things like rock climbing, hunting/fishing, mountain biking, triathlons, and golf; indoor hobbies lean toward working on his house, carpentry, fixing up cars, watching sports, and brewing his own beer.
- **Music**: classic rock, R&B, blues, and/or country
- **Drink**: prefers beer, whiskey, bourbon, and Scotch, neat or on the rocks (wine, champagne, and mixed drinks are just not his thing)
- **Smoke**: may enjoy the occasional cigar, especially when he is celebrating some accomplishment or victory; may dip occasionally,

too (but anything more than a few times a month is a red flag in terms of health and emotional stability)

- **Movies**: His tastes are simple — action, horror, and slapstick comedy; no rom coms, psychodramas, or SciFi for him; all-time favorite film is *"The Shawshank Redemption."*
- **Sex Positions**: on top or bending you over — anything to dominate you in bed
- **Actors who are Athletes**: George Clooney, Daniel Craig, Liam Neeson, Denzel Washington

The Godfather

Before you grab the next tough guy who walks by, you need to know about the shadowy, dark side of the masculine/leader archetype, the Godfather. He will look and energetically feel the same (because he is a masculine/leader, too), but he is different in a few critical ways that make it impossible for you to have a successful marriage with him.

It seems as if the Godfather has the world at his fingertips, but that is not enough. The Godfather is, of course, incredibly masculine and generates tremendous attraction. He also has leadership skills to spare, but there's one critical difference between your Athlete and the Godfather: integrity. Your Athlete has it, while the Godfather doesn't.

The Godfather will bend the rules and cheat to get what he wants. At work, he cuts corners just because others aren't looking and he can get away with it. He also cheats to win, but even then, winning often isn't enough because then he just cheats more to win even bigger.

He may be successful now, but much like the infamous Kenneth Lay, the former CEO of Enron who embezzled millions from the company, or Bernie Madoff, the financial advisor who stole hundreds of millions by selling fake investments, his dishonesty will eventually catch up with him. He may not end up in prison, but you risk losing everything at an important time, such as when the kids go off to college or you are about to retire, because people refuse to do business with him or hire him.

It's not just about being honest today, though. As he earns greater positions of trust and autonomy, he will inevitably face greater opportunity to cheat with increasing stakes, so there is more to gain by cheating. Eventually, any lack of integrity will be tested and found wanting.

Another difference between the Godfather and your Athlete is that the Godfather has even more confidence than your Athlete. The Godfather has so much confidence that he thinks he is special and that the rules don't apply to him — that he is above the rules. Just like the disgraced hotelier, Leona Helmsley, said during her tax evasion trial, "Only the little people pay taxes," the Godfather thinks he is above everyone else and that he can do as he pleases.

Can you see where his lack of integrity comes from now? Psychiatrists have a name for this kind of false sense of superiority: narcissism. Your Athlete has plenty of self-confidence and may walk the edge of arrogance, but he doesn't cross over from healthy self-confidence and self-respect into the delusion of superiority, where he believes that only his plans and desires matter.

However, Godfathers can take another form where their lack of integrity only occurs on a personal level and doesn't seem to show up in their professional lives. You could leave this type of Godfather around $1 million in small bills and not one dollar would go missing, but he still feels that it is somehow okay to lie to his wife and be unfaithful. This disconnection between personal integrity and professional integrity is particularly common in highly successful and powerful men.

Two of American's most admired presidents, Franklin Delano Roosevelt (FDR) and John Fitzgerald Kennedy (JFK), are excellent examples of this disjunction. FDR was re-elected four times and led the U.S. through the two greatest crises of the 20th century, the Great Depression and World War II. He was also married to one of the greatest First Ladies in history, Eleanor Roosevelt, who gave him six children, but that didn't stop him from having numerous affairs during their marriage. He's even rumored to have died of a stroke while in the arms of his mistress.

JFK was even more unfaithful despite being married to one of the most beautiful and beloved women in the world, Jackie Kennedy. He is believed to have had dozens and dozens of affairs, changing mistresses almost like changing clothes. Even Marilyn Monroe didn't rate more than a weekend tryst.

I could go on and on listing powerful men who have strayed, but you get the point.

The problem is that their success and power starts to weaken their integrity by making them think that they have somehow earned the right to an exception from their marriage vows. This weakening of their integrity is complicated by the fact that many women are irresistibly drawn to their success like moths to a flame. It takes incredible integrity and self-control to resist the advances of beautiful women right when a man is starting to age and beginning to doubt his virility, while his marriage has grown comfortable and familiar. Virtually every successful man will face this challenge to some degree if he takes care of his body.

There is only one defense to this constant threat, because there will always be women around who are morally flexible or sufficiently creative in justifying their actions to themselves. Your man must possess a high level of integrity and actively defend your marriage by avoiding risky situations, because we all know what happens to that box of cookies at 2 in the morning when you can't sleep.

How to Spot a Godfather

Here is a quick rundown of my top ways to tell if your masculine leader is a Godfather rather than an Athlete:

1. He cheats at any kind of game other than to let a child win. (Athletes call fouls on themselves in games, even if it means losing.)
2. He runs red lights if no one is around, and not just at 2 a.m. in a dangerous part of town.
3. He fearlessly approached you in public despite you sending out every sign that you didn't want to be approached — sunglasses and headphones on; hair up; no makeup; and eyes locked on your phone, tablet or computer. (Athletes will approach you in public if you seem open to it, but they will respect your "Don't bother me" signs if you don't want to be approached.)
4. In video games, he sets it on the easiest level to win as big as possible. (Athletes set it on the hardest level because they like the challenge.)

5. He tells little lies to make himself look better, not just to make someone else feel better or save them from embarrassment.
6. Your friends tell you he acts as if he is single and that he flirts with other women if you are not around. (Athletes hang out with their guy friends and never flirt with another girl if you are not around.)
7. He brags about breaking rules or getting away with cutting corners.
8. He doesn't respect anyone at his job and thinks they are all stupid and lazy. (Athletes may complain about a single person, but they limit their complaints to a specific problem or issue and don't paint the person as all bad.)
9. He assumes other people are always trying to cheat him or lie to him because he mistakenly assumes everyone lies and cheats like he does.
10. He has actually lied to you about something serious, like a history of having affairs. (Liars and cheaters can change, but much like an addiction, it takes years of treatment and sobriety before you can start to trust him again.)
11. Your friends and family all think he is a bad guy and tell you to dump him. (What are they seeing that you are not?)
12. He has already been unfaithful to you. (Hello! Seriously, what do you need to dump the guy — an intervention?)

If You are Dating a Godfather

If your man does any of these things, you need to take a hard, clear-eyed look at him, if you are not already running for the door as fast as possible. This is when you need to ignore your heart and get into your head. Godfathers are extremely good at hijacking your feelings and using them to overwhelm your awareness and judgment. Your only defense is to do your best to ignore your feelings and use the cold eye of logic to pierce the illusion he has cast.

If you suspect your masculine leader might be a Godfather, you must stop having sex with him if you are to have any hope of regaining a rational perspective and your judgment. Having sex with a man bonds you to him biochemically and changes the wiring in your brain neurologically so you are literally blind to his shortcomings. Sex (and especially orgasms) also cause you to become biochemically addicted to him so leaving him feels like you quit a bad drug habit cold-turkey, but stopping cold turkey is what you have to do, because every time you have sex with him, it is like taking another hit off the crack pipe.

The next step is to stop talking to him so you can think without interference. A Godfather will always tell you what you want to hear. He will apologize and promise to change; whatever it takes to get you to stay. He may even be sincere and want to keep his promise to you to change, but this kind of change takes a complete overhaul of one's heart, mind, and soul. Men often need to lose everything, including you, and have to rebuild their lives from nothing to begin to change at such a deep level.

If he has really gotten into your head, you may have to pull a disappearing act to get away from his influence and clear your head. That means cutting off all contact; don't respond to e-mails, texts, or phone calls. Turn off your phone, since blocking his number won't be enough — he will just borrow a friend's phone to reach you.

No matter how sad and lonely you feel, know that your mind is slowly clearing minute by minute and day by day. If you can last a week with no contact, it will start getting easier and by a month, you will wonder what you saw in him. You may even want to start dating again, but resist the urge to rebound because you are not over him yet.

In the first three months you are apart, you will be very clear about why you had to leave. However, after that, the negative memories and feelings will have faded, while the positive memories and feelings are still relatively strong. The positive memories may cause you to start to question why you left. Again, don't trust your heart. Do your best to remember the full relationship accurately and remind yourself of all the reasons you left.

After six months of no contact, the intensity of the positive feelings will start to fade just like the negative ones. Your recovery will have some legs and you won't be as fragile anymore. Just remember that even though you escaped him, you are still vulnerable to falling for the next Godfather you meet. Many women make the mistake of looking for someone who is different from their ex-Godfather in some superficial way, but who still evokes the same intensity of attraction and feeling.

If you find yourself falling for one Godfather after another, you need more than some advice and a checklist. You need to go to psychotherapy to root out the source of your broken radar and unhealthy attraction. The cause will mostly likely be related to your early childhood (remember the Attachment Styles from Chapter 4?) and your relationship with your parents, so go with a therapist who specializes in psychodynamic psychotherapy (as opposed to cognitive-behavioral psychotherapy). Psychodynamic psychotherapy doesn't work quickly, but very few things can dig deep enough to heal our earliest wounds. Check out Appendix 2 to help you find a psychotherapist.

Attracting Your Athlete

The secret to attracting your Athlete (while screening out the other three archetypes and their shadows) is to require him to approach and pursue you. Yes, I am saying that, as a feminine supporter, you should never initiate or pursue an Athlete. Before you hit the "delete forever" button on your e-reader, please hear me out.

I am not saying this out of some antiquated sense of chivalry. Making him approach and pursue you is a critical test of both his masculinity and leadership. As a feminine supporter, you are best complemented by a masculine leader, so testing him is not some kind of manipulative game. You are merely ensuring that he is a good fit for you. Doing so prevents you from wasting time and protects you from future heartache due to falling in love with someone who is a poor fit.

Requiring him to approach and pursue you also gives you time to see if his masculinity can generate sufficient attraction in you. It also shows you whether he is capable of leading you as a husband and willing to do so. If you make it too easy for him, then down the road, you may find out that he is not masculine enough or a strong enough leader to complement you. In short, you are not playing hard to get here, but rather ensuring that you two will work well together as a couple over the long haul.

Even though you are requiring that he approach and pursue you, that doesn't mean you are passively waiting for him to do everything. There are plenty of things you need to do to attract an Athlete, but it is more like fishing than hunting. You have to choose the right bait, pick a good spot, present the bait properly, and then set the hook at the right moment, instead of jumping in the water and trying to chase the fish down.

Appearance

The male sex drive is primarily visual, so your appearance is critical to attracting your Athlete. Make sure you are dressed attractively. Notice that I didn't say sexy or slutty; that will only draw the unwanted attention of Godfathers, because few things attract them faster than low-hanging fruit. Save the sexy for after you are in an exclusive relationship that is headed toward marriage (and save the slutty for after you are married, to keep things spicy).

The line between attractive and sexy/slutty varies widely from one part of the country to another, so you will have to adapt your look to your locale. One way to know if your look is on point is to look at the types of men who approach you. If you notice that all you tend to attract are Godfathers, then you may want to tone it down a bit. If no one is approaching you at all, then you need to step it up a bit.

If you are strongly feminine this probably isn't too complicated for you. However, if you are moderately feminine, you may need to get your sisters or girlfriends to help you. Just remember: You want him to notice your face, not your makeup.

Also consider growing your hair out. While a short cut can be attractive, short hair tends to be slightly more masculine than long hair. Even though you can compensate by dressing more on the feminine side, short hair can still project enough masculine energy that it can deter Athletes from approaching or pursuing you.

Another important part of your appearance is your figure. No, you don't need to starve yourself to look like the skinny runway models. The fashion industry likes anorexic models because they are walking coat hangers that show off the clothes. Men, on the other hand, actually like a variety of shapes and sizes, but the one consistent physical feature that almost all men find attractive is an hourglass figure where the waist is slightly smaller than the hips and chest.

Instead of starving yourself (anorexia is an awful disease, trust me), you just want to slowly get into a little bit better shape so your waist is slightly smaller than your hips. This advice isn't just for attracting men; it is actually good for your long-term health, too.

In medicine, we refer to this as "the Apple" versus "the Pear" body type. Even if two women have the same height, weight, and percentage of body fat, the Apple who stores her body fat in her abdomen is far less healthy in terms of risk for diabetes, high cholesterol, high blood pressure, heart attacks, and strokes than the Pear who stores her fat in her hips, buttocks, and thighs.

The secret to getting rid of belly fat is not sit-ups (they only strengthen your abdominal muscles). The trick is to follow the right kind of diet and exercise program. If you need to trim your tummy, go download the super-simple, no-willpower diet and exercise plan on my website (www. scottcarrollmd.com) to learn how to lose the belly fat without losing healthy muscle or your feminine shape.

Clearing Blocks and Lowering the Shield

Next, pay attention to the things that block Athletes (but not Godfathers) from approaching you. I'm talking about the unconscious things you're doing that say "Please don't bother me" — things like having your headphones on or intently focusing on a book or your laptop, tablet, or phone when you're out in public spaces.

Similarly, a withdrawn or closed body posture is also perceived by Athletes (but not Godfathers) as an unspoken message that you don't want to be approached. It implies that you will be upset, and they will lose all hope of ever meeting you if they do approach you. Examples of this include having your arms crossed and drawn into your body, while your head is down and you avoid eye contact with everyone around you.

Women unconsciously learn to act this way for a variety of reasons, from your natural human wariness of strangers to being busy trying to get something done, to being in a monogamous relationship, to honestly not wanting any attention. However, the deeper reason most women do this is because they are afraid of being approached and, thus, forced into an uncomfortable situation: namely, having to saying no and disappoint someone. Women in Western culture are often raised to be sensitive to the feelings and desires of others and to especially avoid disappointing others.

This type of socialization against hurting others' feelings comes on top of a natural tendency for females to value relationships and social connections more than males do. The key to overcoming this almost-innate behavior and letting your shield down a bit is noticing when you are about to give in to someone out of fear of upsetting them. Then, instead of giving in, give yourself permission to disappoint them, despite any cultural taboos, and say no politely, but firmly. If you need help with saying no, check out the article on my website (www.scottcarrollmd.com) about saying no with class.

While you want to lower your shield some, you don't want to go to the other extreme, because you still need to create enough of a barrier to keep out the other archetypes. The key to adjusting your shield to the correct level is to pay attention to your behavior in public. Notice whether your body language is open or closed. Try spreading out your body by uncrossing your arms and legs. You don't have to man-spread; just stop tying yourself up in knots. Try leaning back and relaxing to relieve the tension in your body.

Next, take the headphones out of your ears and toss the sunglasses unless you are actually sitting outside in bright sunlight. Let your hair down and put on some light daytime makeup. Ditch the frumpy sweatshirt and wear something cute when you're out and about. Bring a real book or magazine to read instead of your usual electronic gadgets, and hold the cover up so he can see it, because it will give him an easy conversation starter. You never know when your Athlete may appear, so make it a habit to be prepared to meet him whenever you are in public.

Remove any physical barriers that block guys from approaching you. If you are out with friends, sit on the edge of the group instead of the middle, where no one is able to get close to you. Break off from the group by going to the bar or the bathroom alone once in awhile, so Athletes can approach you. Go to coffee shops and bars alone or, if you are meeting friends, get there before they arrive. Sit in an easily accessible place. Avoid corners or booths that make it hard to get near enough to you to talk. Go to quiet, upscale bars where you can have a conversation. Avoid the meat markets. Those places are just prime hunting grounds for Godfathers. Feel free to leave as soon as the band or DJ starts if it's too hard to have a conversation.

Positive Attitude

Once you are comfortable with saying no and with resetting your shield to a reasonable level, you can work on being fully open to someone approaching you. However, to be fully open, you need to cultivate a positive attitude toward anyone and everyone who does approach you. What I mean here is to appreciate everyone's interest in making the effort to meet you, even if you have no interest in dating someone or with being his friend. Instead, think of such men as fans who just want an autograph and maybe a selfie with you.

The next part of having a positive attitude about being approached is to reserve judgment on whether or not a guy is a fan or a date. Not every Athlete will blow you away when you first meet him (in fact, being immediately blown away is often a sign of pathological attraction, which we previously discussed in the chapter on the attachment system). I strongly recommend giving decent guys a second (or even a third) chance to see if they can generate some chemistry. The only guys you shouldn't give a second chance are the ones with whom you spot a red flag.

Additional Barriers

After you become emotionally open to being approached and start doing things to make it easier for men to approach you, you need to take a look at your friends and family to see if any of them block good men from approaching you. These types of barriers can take a variety of forms, such as your over-protective girlfriend who won't let a strange man speak to you. It also includes mean girlfriends who glare at every guy that approaches, but the worst one is the slut who steals every guy who tries to talk to you.

If you notice that no one approaches you when you are out with certain girlfriends, try going out without them. A true wingman helps you meet guys. They will initiate a conversation with a cute guy and then bring you into the conversation while they bow out. If they meet a guy, they will bring him over to meet you. Most importantly, they never outshine you or try to steal a guy. That's a tall order to live up to as a wingman, so it shouldn't be too hard to figure out who's a wingman and who's just a block.

Another barrier to finding your Athlete is being impatient. Many women decide they are finally ready to meet the One and jump right in by going out a lot and joining a bunch of online dating websites. However, when they don't meet him right away, they get frustrated and completely stop looking. Instead, you need to accept that it will probably take some time to find your Athlete and to make a consistent effort, rather than the typical hot-and-cold approach many women take.

Part of making a consistent effort also means going on a lot of first dates (and second and third dates) with guys who are not your Athlete. Even though my wife almost set a record by meeting me only two weeks after joining an online dating website, she still had to go on four lousy first dates before we met. On the other hand, I was online for about a year and a half and went on dozens and dozens of dates with many wonderful women who were not the One before I met my wife.

The last barrier I want to address here is the resistance some women have to online dating. Basically, if you are over 30 years old, you absolutely have to get online if you are serious about finding your Athlete. Heck, if you are over 25 years old and not in school, you should be online. However, covering all of the things you need to know to date online effectively would almost double the length of this book, but you can download a free copy of my online dating e-book, Meeting Your Athlete Online on my website.

Best Five Places to Meet an Athlete

Let's count down the best five ways to meet your Athlete in real life.

5) Join a golf club or take golf lessons, then stay for a drink at the golf course clubhouse.
4) Go to a sports bar on weekends in the fall during any big football games (or any major sporting events like the World Series or March Madness). The place will be packed with athletes, but few single females, placing the odds solidly in your favor.
3) Go to a happy hour where all the young professionals in your area go (ask around to find out). Go regularly by yourself or with your wingman to increase your odds.

2) Join an upscale sports club or gym where you can get in shape and join their intramural sports leagues (he might be a serious amateur athlete).

1) Attend meetings such as conferences or local meetings of professional groups such as the Chamber of Commerce or bar association.

Now that you have the technical knowledge to identify your Athlete (and avoid a Godfather), we will kick it up a notch and teach you how to induce the entire universe to conspire to bring your Athlete to your doorstep. Skip to Chapter 11 to learn how to manifest him energetically.

CHAPTER EIGHT

The Engineer

The Engineer is masculine, tends to love technology, and is smart. He is also more logical than emotional and seeks the emotional spark missing in his life, which is why he is drawn to your passion and sensitivity. He is also successful and makes good money at work, but doesn't have the desire to lead in his personal life and would rather save his leadership energy for work. Don't be surprised if his personal life is a bit dull and in need a makeover.

This is where you come in. Your leadership will supply the spark to turn the deadwood of his personal life into a blazing fire. He is probably a bit shy and uncomfortable socially — basically a nerd at heart — even if he is gorgeous and in amazing shape. Your passion and energy will spice up his life and you will lead him on adventures he has never dreamed of. Most importantly, he will love how you connect him to other people without trying to fight you for the lead.

Your challenge is to not look past him because he is quiet and mistakenly go for the shiny masculine leader. Masculine leaders will be drawn to you and will often approach you with little prompting, which you kind of like, but your own need to lead will inevitably clash with his. You may be tempted to repress your need to lead so you don't appear threatening and chase him away, but it will still come out indirectly, no matter what you do, and cause screaming arguments over the littlest things. Resist the urge to go for the shiny costume jewelry and hold out for solid gold.

How can you tell if a man is a masculine supporter? First, he won't approach you in a bold way and will especially have trouble approaching you while you are in the middle of your group of friends, because that requires initiation and confidence, which are core leadership skills he lacks. He may start a conversation by making a comment to you if you happen to be standing next to him in line somewhere, but generally, you will have to give him permission in some form and maybe a little encouragement before he'll stick his neck out.

Another clue is his choice of career. Given his love of technology and mechanical things, he may literally be an engineer or a scientist. He may also work with computers as a network analyst or programmer. He could also be in finance on the research side as an analyst (not sales) or work as an accountant in a major corporation. Alternatively, he could be old-school and work as a mechanic, welder, plumber, or electrician (they make more money than you think). The key is that he works with things — devices, money or machines — not people.

You can also spot an Engineer by his gadgets. He'll have the latest smartphone, possibly two, but in a very uncool belt holder. If you run into him during the daytime, he'll have the latest tablet or super-thin laptop. However, the killer gadget that absolutely proves he's an Engineer is a smart watch, especially if he spent more on it than on his car. He loves to talk about his gadgets, too, so be prepared to gently change the subject and lead the conversation to something more interesting.

Just as with the Athlete (masculine leader), he will be protective if he senses you are in physical danger, but won't try to stifle or control you. He will tend to be chivalrous and pull chairs out for you, but then may apologize and ask if you like such things. However, once you have given him permission, he'll be chivalrous to a fault, so don't hesitate to tell him if he's overdoing it.

Don't be put off if he is not religious or spiritual like you. Given his strong preference for logic over feelings or faith, he will probably be an atheist or an agnostic, if he even thinks about spirituality much at all. However, he will follow your lead about going to church or synagogue and be happy to bring your children. Just don't expect him to actually believe.

The best example of what your Engineer and your marriage to him should look like is the marriage of Sheryl Sandberg and the late Dave Goldberg, who died in 2015 in a freak treadmill accident. Sheryl is, of course, the author of *Lean In* and the chief operating officer of Facebook, while Dave was an executive at Yahoo when they first met and CEO of Survey Monkey at the time of his tragic death.

I don't know either of them personally, but Sheryl provided a window into their marriage in her book, *Lean In*, and from her public talks about how they shared parenting and household responsibilities equally. Even though she never explicitly says it, you can tell that she was the leader in their relationship and that he was the strong, supportive presence behind her shining public star. Regardless, she knew he was the perfect man for her. In her book, she implores women to make the best decision possible in whom you marry.

If you still doubt why a Engineer makes such a great husband for you as a feminine leader consider this: They will not argue with you over what to do together and prefer to compromise instead. They tend to have stable, good-paying jobs with health insurance and retirement plans. They don't spend a lot of time drinking at the bar with their buddies. They work hard at helping you achieve your dreams and goals. They are patient parents and father smart children (IQ is largely genetic). Finally, they can either fix everything that breaks in your house or at least hire and supervise the best person to fix it.

The Ultimate Engineer

Here is a sample profile of an Engineer to help create an image in your mind's eye so you will know him when you see him:

- **Age**: about your age (no more than five years younger or older than you)
- **Grooming**: short hair, but probably needs a haircut; may have a beard that needs a trim and to have the hair on his neck cleaned up
- **Height**: your height to much taller than you (just not shorter)

- **Build**: fit and lean, more into aerobic exercise like running and cycling than weight lifting (again, no potbellies because they are a sign of poor health in a male and of an early death)
- **Clothing**: functional and simple, likely just a T-shirt and jeans, since he doesn't think about such things much beyond function (beware if his clothes are dirty or smell — that is a red flag that he is actually the shadow of an Engineer, a Gamer)
- **Accessories**: either a fancy smart watch or no watch at all (he uses his phone); no piercings, flashy rings, or tattoos; just the latest smartphone or two, probably in an uncool belt holder
- **Hats**: none unless it is really sunny, then a wide-brimmed panama that doesn't match his outfit (did I mention he's more into function than style?)
- **Shoes**: probably sneakers or pseudo-dress shoes with comfortable soles; if it is summer, you know you are on the right track if he's got on sandals — bonus points if he's wearing socks with his sandals (don't worry, he will let you dress him better once you are married)
- **Hobbies**: outdoors — limited to running, hiking, and road bicycling; indoors — may be a bit unusual, such as model trains, building and flying drones, collecting science fiction memorabilia, or restoring old computers
- **Music**: unusual tastes, such as classical, big band, or bluegrass.
- **Drink**: prefers mixed drinks and cider because he doesn't like the taste of beer or hard alcohol.
- **Smoke**: never smokes and can quote all the statistics on how bad smoking is for you
- **Movies**: science fiction, with an occasional kung fu or Bond flick thrown in; all-time favorite: the original "Star Wars" from 1977, even if he wasn't born yet
- **Sex**: eager to please, whether it is you on top or going down on you
- **Actors who are Engineers**: Jeff Goldblum, Zach Braff, and Benedict Cumberbatch

The Gamer

Before you grab the next nerd who walks by, you need to know about the shadowy, dark side of the masculine supporter archetype: the Gamer. He will look and energetically feel the same (because he is a masculine supporter), but he is different in a few critical ways that make it impossible for you to have a successful marriage with him.

He's just as smart and masculine as the Engineer, but he uses technology or his hobbies to avoid dealing with some aspect of his life. Basically, he's either obsessed with or addicted to some activity that will seriously interfere with his career, his relationships, or both.

Notice that it doesn't necessarily have to be video games that he is obsessed with. Any obsessive interest or focus can be the problem, from collecting baseball cards to restoring vintage cars to hunting and fishing; anything that crosses the line from a being a wholesome hobby into something problematic.

You will know that his hobby is a problem because he will be late for or even miss important events because he "lost track of time" while he was doing his hobby. He will miss what you are saying because he is thinking about his hobby. He'll ask to borrow money to pay some bill because he spent too much on his hobby this month. He'll invite you to go on vacation some place, but there's a convention related to his hobby going on there at the same time.

When you confront him about it, he either angrily denies that his hobby is a problem or he promises to change but then doesn't follow through. Then he starts hiding the time he spends and sneaks around to engage in his hobby. He may try to cut back if you push him hard enough, but he eventually loses control and goes on a binge. When you drag him away from his hobby, he is anxious and doesn't know what to do with himself. If you've been together a while, you may get the feeling you are raising a son more than dating a man. Any of these behaviors should be a major red flag and send you running for the door.

Spotting the Gamer

Here are my top five clues for spotting a Gamer:

5) He pulls "all nighters" to play games or engage in any activity that is not required for his primary job.
4) He owns both an Xbox and a PlayStation or is restoring more than one vehicle at a time.
3) He has an entire room devoted to his "hobby."
2) He spends more than 10% of what he earns on his "hobby."
1) He speaks fluent Klingon (seriously!)

However, the he biggest red flag you need to watch for is his little problem with Internet porn. I'm not talking about you enjoying some porn together to get you in the mood. I'm talking about him staying up at night and sneaking behind your back to watch it, despite your fabulous sex life. Such behavior poses a major risk to your relationship. After being so emotionally unfaithful, how long do you think it will take before watching is not enough?

If you end up with a Gamer by mistake, you must first accept that he cannot be the husband you desire, no matter how much potential he may have. Accept that he has a hole in his heart that your love cannot fill. Also accept that only by completely and permanently breaking up with him can you open yourself to receiving the amazing relationship you deserve.

Recognize that, just as with an addict, staying with him merely enables him to continue and to avoid having to change. Only by breaking up with him can he hit rock bottom and possibly begin to heal his heart. Just know that he will need years of "sobriety" before he can begin to recover — far longer than you can or should wait.

Attracting Your Engineer

As I said at the beginning of this chapter, the Engineer won't approach you while you are in the middle of your group of friends. At most, he may make a comment to you if you happen to be standing next to him waiting in line, but generally you will have to give him permission in some form to approach you. (If a man approaches you before you've given him permission, you are probably dealing with an Athlete or Film Director and need to reject him.)

You don't want to approach him, because you need to make sure he is sufficiently masculine to be a good match for you: Masculine energy naturally pursues what it desires. This is an important test to make sure he complements properly you and doesn't lean too much to the feminine side. You also need him to be able to lead and initiate at least occasionally, especially if you are only a moderate leader.

The one exception to the "help him but let him approach you" method is if you are a super-strong leader (10 or 11 on the leadership spectrum). If you are comfortable or, better yet, prefer to lead in almost every area of your personal life and your future relationship, you can approach him. However, be sure you really do want to lead all the time, because if you approach and pursue him, you are setting the pattern for how the two of you will relate for the rest of your relationship.

Otherwise you will need to give him permission and possibly a little encouragement to approach you such as flirting with him. To flirt with him, all you have to do is briefly make eye contact (3 seconds is sufficient), smile, and then look down. After about 10 seconds, look back up, make eye contact, and smile again briefly before you look away.

If he doesn't come over and introduce himself, give him one more chance a few minutes later. If he still doesn't come over at that point, there is something wrong, such as he is too feminine or he's not available for some reason. Just let it go and move on.

I know this all seems kind of manipulative, but think of it as if you were hiring someone for a technical position. You would obviously have specific job requirements, such as an education level in a specific field, along with a certain amount of experience. After all, you wouldn't hire a biologist to design your computer network if he didn't have any training in computers. Similarly, taking this approach screens out all the men who just won't fit well with you. It doesn't mean they aren't good men or that they won't make a good husband for someone; they just wouldn't make a good husband for you.

If you are using a wingman when you go out, just make sure your wingman is actually trying to help you meet someone. No matter what she says, you have to watch her actions carefully to make sure she isn't actually blocking you or stealing the best ones from you. You also need to make sure she knows how to correctly identify an Engineer and how to screen out Gamers.

If you are on an online dating website, only wink at or poke him (whatever method the website uses to get him to notice your profile), but don't actually send him an e-mail or message. Remember that you want him to pursue you after you give him permission. Whatever you do, don't start messaging cute guys. Masculine leaders will let you pursue them, but only for a hookup and not to actually start a relationship. A positive response to your initial e-mail or message isn't necessarily good for you in the long term.

Speaking of online dating, there is a lot you need to know to be successful, but covering it here would vastly increase the length of this book. Instead, go to my website to download a copy of my online dating e-book, Meeting Your Engineer Online. If you are over 30 years old and not online, then you are not serious about meeting someone. In fact, unless you are completely surrounded by eligible Engineers at school or work, you need to be online no matter how old you are.

Appearance

The male sex drive is primarily visual and Engineers still lean to the masculine side, so your appearance is an important part of attracting him. Make sure you are dressed nicely, but not slutty or too sexy. They just attract the wrong type of men.

If you are strongly feminine, then this probably isn't too complicated for you. However, if you are moderately feminine, you may need to get your sisters or girlfriends to help you. Watch the makeup and keep it light and tasteful. Just remember: You want him to notice your face, not your makeup. Consider growing your hair out, since long hair is more feminine. Jeans and shorts are fine for the daytime, but go for dresses and skirts at night.

Another important part of your appearance is your figure. No, you don't need to starve yourself to look like the skinny runway models. The fashion industry prefers anorexic-looking models because they show off the clothes better, but men actually like a variety of shapes and sizes. However, the one consistent physical feature that almost all men prefer, including Engineers, is an hourglass figure where your waist is smaller than your hips and bust.

Instead of going on some type of aggressive diet or exercise program, you just want to get into a little bit better shape so your waist is slightly smaller than your hips. This advice isn't just for attracting men; it is also good for your long-term health.

In medicine, we refer to this as the "Apple" and "Pear" body types. Even if two women have the same, height, weight, and percentage of body fat, the Apple who stores her body fat in her abdomen is far less healthy in terms of risk for diabetes, high cholesterol, high blood pressure, heart attacks, and strokes than the Pear who stores her fat in her hips, buttocks, and thighs.

The secret to getting rid of belly fat is not sit-ups (they only strengthen your abdominal muscles). It is to follow the right kind of diet and exercise program. If you need to trim your tummy, go download my super-simple, no-willpower diet and exercise plan on my website (www.scottcarrollmd.com) to learn how to lose the belly fat without losing healthy muscle or your feminine shape.

Working a Room

When you are out in public or at any kind of function, including ones for work, take a moment to survey the room. Similarly to when you are networking, notice the men who are likely candidates: good looking, the right age range, tall enough, sociable but not a butterfly that is flitting around the room. He may be in a group, but he's the quieter one on the edge, not the leader at the center.

After you have identified a likely target, wait in an easily accessible place where he can see you, but not anywhere he would have an easy excuse to stand next to you such as in a line or next to the bar or the hors d'oeuvres. The point of this is to test him and see if he automatically approaches you before you give him permission or encouragement. Obviously, if he does approach you or anyone else he doesn't know, cross him off your list because he's some type of leader, not the supportive type that would best complement you.

If he hasn't approached you after several minutes of just sitting or standing there, clearly in his line of sight, start flirting with him as I described previously. If the flirting works and he approaches you, try to get to know him a little bit. Your goal is to draw him out and get him to talk about what he does for a living, his "hobbies", and his preferences in film and music. These simple questions should give you a good idea of whether he is an Engineer, a Gamer, or some other type of male.

If he appears to be an Engineer, start turning on the charm. Remember, your vivaciousness is what is going to draw him in and spur him to throw caution to the wind to pursue you. You can caress his arm and stare deeply into his eyes, whatever you want short of asking for his digits or to meet again. You can roll out the red carpet for him, but he has to walk down it on his own.

If he is not an Engineer, politely excuse yourself and find another likely target to check out. Most guys will accept a polite blow-off, but if he doesn't play along, you may need to say no more firmly. As a leader, you may be perfectly comfortable saying no to someone, but if you are not, check out the article on my website for my four-step process to master saying no firmly with class and compassion (http://www.scottcarrollmd.com/saying-no-with-class/).

Handling Rejection

Since you will be putting yourself out there to engage specific men by flirting, you run the risk of being rejected. If you are a super-strong leader, you are probably not inclined to second-guessing or beating yourself up, but if you are, here's how to handle it.

First, you must accept that you do not actually know why he didn't come over. You don't have all the facts, so you cannot say for sure why. Assuming that he didn't come over because he didn't like the way you looked would be a logical error. The actually reason could have simply been that he was in a serious relationship and wasn't available.

My point is that you can determine nothing from a single episode because you don't have enough data. Agonizing over why he didn't approach you is pointless and a waste of time. You must mentally reject that line of thought and consciously chose to replace it with the logical thought that you don't really know so you can let it go. This process is a mental skill that will seem awkward at first, but if you keep practicing it, you will get better and better until you start doing it automatically without any effort. This will make the dating process much easier for you, especially since attracting an Engineer means you must set yourself up to be pursued in a way that may take a bit of repetition to work.

However, if you keep struggling with this or can't seem to get started at all, you have two options. You can buy and read the book *Feeling Good* by David Burns, MD, or you can start going to a psychotherapist who specializes in cognitive behavioral therapy (CBT). I recommend giving the book a try first, because even if the book doesn't work, it will prime you to make faster progress with the therapist. It's also much cheaper than actual therapy. You can pick up a copy at almost any used-book store or online for just a few dollars. You can also check out Appendix 2 at the end of this book for tips on how to find a good therapist.

That said, if you are literally getting no one to come over after you flirt a minimum of five times, then run over your list in your mind to see if you are missing something: attractive feminine dress, light makeup, feminine figure where your waist is smaller than your hips, limiting eye contact to 3 seconds when you flirt, smiling when you make eye contact, etc. If everything seems to be in place and you are not in a gay bar or a couple's event, keep going, because dating tends to be a bit of a numbers game.

If you continue to strike out, ask your wingman or system buddy to see if she can spot the problem. It helps if she was actually there and could see who you were trying to flirt with and what you were wearing and doing. You may have to encourage her to be honest, since most female friends don't want to hurt your feelings. If she makes any suggestion at all for you to change something, go with it even if it doesn't feel right. Remember, we all tend to have blind spots when it comes to self-awareness.

If what she suggests actually upsets you, then that is an even stronger sign that she is on the right path. Unconsciously, you already know the answer, but it threatens you emotionally in some way, which is why you didn't think of it on your own. She will tell you that your favorite earrings are hideous or that your makeup is wrong. She may also tell you that your outfit is frumpy or doesn't work for you. Of course, the most painful, but true, advice she may give is that you need to get into better shape.

You may be angry and upset at first, but understand that if there were no truth whatsoever to what she said, you would merely be puzzled about why she said that. Your strong emotional reaction is proof that she is at least partially right. You now have the choice to accept it so you will be able to do something about it or keep lying to yourself and never solve the problem. Ask yourself, do you want to be right or be in love?

Five Best Places to Meet an Engineer

Let's count down the five best places to meet your Engineer:

5) Your local Unitarian church
4) Good coffee shops near any tech companies or large employers
3) Running, bicycling, or tennis clubs in your area
2) Sports club or gym (he'll be in the back of the spin class)
1) Professional meetings and technical conferences (or hotel bars when conferences are in town)

Now that you know how to attract your Engineer (and avoid his shadow, the Gamer), we are going to super-charge your ability to attract him by teaching you how to induce the entire universe to conspire to bring him to you. Skip to Chapter 11 to learn how to energetically manifest your Engineer.

CHAPTER NINE

The Film Director

*C*alling a man feminine is not an insult of some kind; rather, it describes his approach to the world. For example, feminine men are in touch with their feelings and often feel their way through problems rather than only using logic to solve them. They are more aware of other people's feelings and thus relate well to others. They can also be good with children because they are naturally patient and nurturing. Another clue that a man leans to the feminine side is if he is creative. Creativity is a highly feminine trait because it requires access to one's feelings and intuition.

Where this gets interesting is when you combine strong leadership personality traits with creativity. The Film Director possesses this rare combination, which allows him to have vision and then to persuade and organize others to achieve his vision. While he may not be a real film director, he is likely engaged in a creative or nurturing endeavor that involves organizing others, such as being an orchestra conductor, choir director, lead architect at a design firm, psychotherapy supervisor, or elementary school principal.

Alternatively, he may not work in a creative or nurturing field, but he leads the group of volunteers that plan and organize his community's annual music festival. The point is to look for signs of creativity or nurturing combined with a leadership role somewhere in his life.

Another way to tell if a man is relating to you through his feminine side is how he communicates with you. For example, when you are explaining a problem or describing a stressful, upsetting situation, he really listens and asks how you feel, rather than cutting you off to tell you how to solve it. You may also be drawn to his sweetness and kindness, and how he takes care of you and makes you comfortable.

You will see signs of his leadership in his social life, too. He will plan wonderful events, such as throwing parties and organizing benefits, along with planning fun activities for your dates that he knows you will enjoy. He will also be spontaneous and think of amazing things to do on the spur of the moment. His natural creativity and fearless ability to initiate and organize others makes the Film Director one of the most exciting kind of guy to be around.

Your challenge in this type of relationship is to appreciate his sweetness and sensitivity while you take a more logical, laid-back approach as a masculine supporter. One of your most important roles in your relationship with him is to protect him from people who try to take advantage of his kindness. You may also need to watch the budget, because he can be a bit loose with money, especially when he is in his creative flow.

The Ultimate Film Director

Here is a sample profile of a Film Director to help create an image in your mind's eye, so you will know him when you see him:

- **Age**: about 5 to 10 years older (but no more than 15 years older, and never younger than you)
- **Grooming**: long and stylish hair or shaved head (no combovers or pony tails with bald spots)
- **Height**: 6 inches shorter to 6 inches taller than you
- **Build**: fit with a thin to medium build, even though he doesn't go to the gym much because he's so busy running around doing things
- **Clothing**: flashy and artistic; the man knows how to dress
- **Accessories**: almost anything goes, from piercings to tattoos to multiple rings

- **Hats**: only if it is part of his look
- **Shoes**: Italian and nicer than yours, with a bit of heel
- **Hobbies**: loves the arts, from going to museums to ballet to indie films; loves to travel and wants to visit all the amazing cities and natural wonders of the world
- **Music**: has a refined and varied taste, from opera to pop to international; drawn to soulful voices and creative fusions of genres
- **Drink**: a connoisseur of fine wines and aperitifs
- **Smoke**: may sneak a natural cigarette here and there, but generally tries to refrain
- **Movies**: loves old movies and thinks most of the new ones are garbage, but then can't resist watching the Oscars
- **Sex**: will take charge and make you feel things you never knew were possible
- **Actors who are Film Directors**: Johnny Depp, Johnny Depp, Johnny Depp (did I forget to mention Johnny Depp?)

The Rock Star

Let's talk for a moment about the shadowy, dark side of the feminine/leader archetype, the Rock Star. He will look and energetically feel the same (because he is a feminine/leader), but he is different in a few critical ways that make him a poor choice for a husband.

The Rock Star is what happens when the Film Director uses his considerable leadership, sensitivity, and creativity for his personal pleasure and enjoyment rather than to work and create for the good of others. Just like a real rock star, he would rather party, do drugs, sleep with a lot of women, and generally shirk responsibility instead of living up to his potential.

You will have to be discerning to tell if a man is a Film Director or a Rock Star. The most important thing to look for is whether he smokes regularly or uses drugs. Regular smoking or drug use clearly indicates that a man is more focused on his personal comfort and pleasure than his accomplishments or commitments (or his health). Such men lack the necessary motivation and self-discipline to accomplish long-term goals like having a successful career or raising a family.

However, there are times where a feminine leader can go either way. He may party a bit too much and be a bit of a player, but he can clean up with some tough love and the right motivation. The key is that you have to be able to walk away if he slips up and doesn't hold up his end of the bargain. To do this, your head has to be firmly in charge instead of your heart. Otherwise, steer clear and avoid any hint of a Rock Star you sense in a man.

The second key difference between the Film Director and his shadow, the Rock Star, is integrity. Similarly to the Athlete and his shadow, the Godfather, integrity is critical for both marriage and long-term career success. If a man is not honest and straight up with people or cuts corners at work or in business, people eventually figure it out and refuse to hire him or work with him.

In relationships, any lack of integrity can lead to cheating and infidelity. As a man gains higher and higher levels of success, he will attract the inappropriate attention of bored and lonely women with limited self-awareness and poor self-control. There will always be one or two hanging around who are enamored with his success, power, wealth, fame, brilliance, or vivaciousness and can't help themselves.

All throughout history, lonely young women with daddy issues have thrown themselves at married men because of their accomplishments. Don't assume you can spot them or keep them away from your man, because they are generally nice young women and not obvious problem children. The only defense against them is for your Film Director to have impeccable integrity so that he prides his word above all else and will honor his marriage vows just like he would a million-dollar deal sealed with a handshake.

How can you tell if your man has the integrity to be a Film Director or is just a Rock Star? One clue is that the Rock Star thinks he is special and that the rules don't apply to him. He thinks he is above everyone else and that he can do as he pleases. He is narcissistic and has delusions of superiority — he believes that only his plans and desires matter and that he can do whatever he wants without regard for the consequences or impact on others.

Another clue is that he justifies his actions by claiming everyone else is cheating and is dishonest, so he has to cheat to level the playing field. He actually believes he is merely fighting fire with fire and not taking advantage of other people. If you really want to understand the twisted logic such men use to justify their actions, go watch Oprah's 2013 interview of Lance Armstrong.

How to Spot a Rock Star

Here are some tips to help you tell if your feminine leader is a Rock Star and not the Film Director you're looking for:

1. He cheats without a good reason.
2. He cuts corners whenever he thinks he won't get caught.
3. He brags about how he got away with cheating or cutting corners.
4. He exaggerates his accomplishments to make himself look better even though he has nothing to be ashamed of.
5. You or your friends catch him flirting with other women.
6. He doesn't respect the other people in his field and claims all of their successes were due to luck, not earned or deserved.
7. He assumes other people are always trying to cheat him or lie to him because he mistakenly assumes everyone cheats and lies just like he does.
8. You were the other woman he cheated with during his last relationship.
9. Your friends and family all think he is a con artist and tell you to dump him.
10. He has been unfaithful to you, lied to you or stole from you. (Seriously, what does it take to get you to dump a guy?)

If your man does any of these things, you should run for the door and not try to change him, understand him, or make excuses for him. This is when you need to ignore your heart and get into your head. Rock Stars are extremely good at hijacking your feelings and using them to manipulate you. Your only defense is to do your best to ignore your feelings and be as logical as possible so your masculine side can save you.

If you suspect your Film Director might actually be a Rock Star, you must stop having sex with him. Even though your masculine side is stronger than your feminine side, you are still a woman and having sex with a man bonds you to him biochemically and makes it harder for you to see his shortcomings. The bonding also makes it hard to leave him because leaving can feel like you are trying to kick a bad drug habit. Do yourself a favor and put down the crack pipe.

The next step is cut off contact with him so he can't wear down your determination to leave. There is no point in talking to him because he is just going to tell you what you want to hear. He will be contrite and promise to change if only you will stay. He may even be sincere and want to keep his promise to you to change, but this kind of change takes a complete overhaul, and few Rock Stars have it in them to dig this deep and stick with the program.

Lying and cheating others is actually addicting and has to be treated much like an addiction. If he is sincere about his desire to change, then the best thing you can do for him is to break up with him so he can be alone to work on it. After all, if you have an alcohol problem and you work as a bartender, the first step to getting sober is to change your career.

To get away from such a manipulative person, you have to ghost him: Don't respond to e-mails, texts or phone calls. You should only answer your phone if your family or a close friend who hated him calls (and they know you're ghosting him) because he will borrow someone's phone or get a new number. You will need to continue to ghost him until you've completed the grieving process, if not permanently.

At first, you may feel incredibly sad, but know you are letting go and healing with every tear you shed and with every lonely night. If you can last a week, it will start getting easier. By a month, the sadness will start to lift. Just don't start dating again yet, because you may be more fragile than you realize. Rock Stars are notorious for messing with your heart and mind to make you more vulnerable to their manipulations, and it takes time to heal that kind of damage.

Three months is the minimum amount of time people typically need to heal from this type of breakup, but don't be shocked if it takes as long as six months. Just don't relax your guard, because the negative feelings can fade before the positive ones and he can manipulate you into taking him back more easily during this phase.

If you keep falling for Rock Stars or feel like you are a Rock Star magnet, you need more than some advice and a checklist. You need to go to psychotherapy to root out the source of your broken radar. The cause will mostly likely be due to your early childhood and your relationship with your parents, so go with a therapist who specializes in psychodynamic psychotherapy (as opposed to cognitive-behavioral). Psychodynamic psychotherapy doesn't work quickly, but very few things can dig deep enough to heal our earliest wounds. Check out Appendix 2 for tips on how to find a good therapist.

Attracting Your Film Director

How do you attract a rare bird like the Film Director? First, he may not try to approach you because he is too busy chasing more feminine women whom he mistakenly thinks are right for him. To catch a man who is not even looking in your direction, you must be friends first and then see if the relationship catches fire.

Your job is to get close to him and become his friend. You should take every opportunity to casually hang out with him to see if there is a spark. Remember, he is still a man and a leader, so he must be allowed to pursue you. If you pursue him, he's too likely to see you as his "woman on the side" while he swings for the fences with more feminine women who are wrong for him.

Instead, help him with his various projects. Your logical and practical masculine perspective will enable you to see gaps and flaws he won't notice. You will also likely be much better at the financial side and can figure out how to get his projects funded or, more importantly, how he could make money from his creative endeavors. Your goal is to show him that you will dramatically enhance both his career and life, and not to try to be the shiny arm-candy he usually goes for. In short, show him you're different — an equal partner, not the flavor of the month.

Again, don't initiate anything romantic; just let him see what you bring to the table. Making him pursue you ensures that he is all in and wants a committed relationship, not just a friendship with benefits or another sex buddy.

As feminine leaders, Film Directors can seduce women in ways their masculine counterparts have never even dreamed of, without ever having to deceive them about wanting a relationship. That is why you will need to play a little hard to get to make sure he really wants a committed relationship and not something casual.

Don't worry about getting stuck in the friend zone, the way women often do with men. Men are different. If they like you, they like you and will go for you, friendship be damned.

Appearance

Your appearance is not as important for attracting your Film Director as it is for the other archetypes, but it is not irrelevant, either. Even though he takes a feminine approach to life, he is still a man, so there is a visual component to attracting him. You just need to keep yourself fit and muscular, which is highly sexy in its own way, so hit the gym and get buff. Hang out with the body builders so they can show you proper technique and share dieting techniques that build muscle while cutting fat.

Just watch the supplements, since some of them contain massive amounts of caffeine and other dangerous stimulants, as well as creatine, which can damage your kidneys. In fact, you don't need supplements beyond a healthy, balanced diet; a multivitamin; and a few cups of black coffee or unsweetened tea.

In addition to hitting the gym, consider taking up a martial art. Don't worry about becoming too strong or tough. With the Film Director, this is just the right touch to make you stand out as a woman unlike any he's ever known. Just think of yourself as his female bodyguard who is always ready to pull him out of danger. There is something irresistibly sexy about being with a woman who can break you in two if you tick her off. This kind of fitness is also good for scaring off the groupies who come sniffing around your man.

Stop reading Cosmo and those other girly magazines and dress to show off your muscles. Instead of low-cut blouses and skirts, go for sleeveless tops and tight pants. You probably don't even need to wear much, if any, makeup. The one exception here is that you should still wear heels, even if it means you look him in the eye or even tower over him. Again, there is something incredibly sexy about being with a woman who can look down at you.

Don't worry too much about your hair — just keep it simple and easy to take care of. Color it if you need to, but a short, stylish cut that shows off your jawline is perfect for you.

Where to Meet Him

Unlike the other archetypes, you will not be able to meet the Film Director in a bar or other social venue, or even online. There will just be too much eye-candy hanging around for him to try to seduce. Even if he did approach you, it would just be for a hookup and not anything serious.

What's a strong women like you to do? You need to meet him on different grounds where you have the advantage naturally.

In your case, that means in artistic settings such as an art gallery or film opening where he is creatively engaged and isn't just working his seduction game. Yes, there will still be plenty of eye-candy walking around, but he will be there for the artistic and creative experience, not just to get lucky. Your job is to engage him intelligently. Study up on whatever event you are going to so you can ask good questions and make thoughtful comments.

Don't be put off if he has some hot young thing with him because Film Directors always have arm-candy. To him, arm-candy is just like any other accessory and is simply part of his look. Remember, the arm-candy was chosen for her ability to make him look good, not for anything deeper. You don't need to perceive her as a threat or even as competition. In fact, you can basically ignore her and focus on him. Just be ready with your death stare if she protests or interrupts.

Keep your first meeting professional and don't try to pick him up or go home with him. You are just trying to make an impression and get into his head a little bit. You want to give him the sense that you see right through his game and aren't interested in such trivial things — you may be fine talking about art with him, but you will never be one of his playthings.

Don't feel bad if he turns it on with the arm-candy right in front of you. He's just trying to make you feel jealous and trick you into playing his game. Don't fall for it, even if he takes the arm-candy home and not you. Keep cool and be satisfied with that for now, while he may be with her, he is imagining being with you.

You should always carry a business card or have some other professional way for your Film Director to contact you later if he asks. Don't be surprised if he doesn't ask the first time you meet. Just keep going to the same kinds of artistic and creative events. You will run into him again, because he goes to lots of such events.

When you do run into him again, strike up a meaningful conversation about the art or the event again without a hint of flirtation. In fact, the more you seem to be there for the art, the better.

The best types of events to go to are ones where his work is being featured. Just be prepared to discuss and critique his work meaningfully. You want to balance any compliments with constructive criticism that could help him make it better. Of course, the killer move is to suggest a way he could market or sell his work better. Don't be surprised if he calls you the next day to discuss your ideas.

Now you have your opportunity to be his friend and give him a taste of how you will enhance his life far more than the arm-candy he normally wastes his time with. As I said earlier, don't initiate anything and be prepared to play hard to get to make him demonstrate his commitment to pursuing you.

Of course, the best clue that he is serious about pursuing you is if he dumps all of his arm-candy and other assorted toys. However, most Film Directors won't automatically jump into the deep end of the pool. They will try to test the water first. That is when you must stand absolutely firm and demand that he get rid of his entire harem before you will go on a single date with him. This is also when you must make it clear that you have a zero-tolerance policy for unfaithfulness and that you will never forgive any form of cheating. You don't want him to think he has a mulligan in his back pocket.

I know this is a tough stance to take, and he may walk away because of it, but if he can't accept your terms, he may be teetering too close to being a Rock Star and you are better off letting him go. After all, do you really want to have to remember how he betrayed you every time you have sex with him for the rest of your life? I have met elderly women who still have bouts of rage at their husbands for a single indiscretion from 40 years ago.

If he walks away, comfort yourself with the knowledge that no matter what, you have your self-respect. There is no greater betrayal than to betray yourself by allowing someone to mistreat and abuse you. Besides, there is always a chance he will miss you so much that he will eventually come back and accept your terms. Just don't wait for him for more than a few months — and even then, you should be working on other prospects.

Handling Rejection

Since you will be putting yourself out there trying to engage your Film Director, you run the risk of rejection. The good news is that when it comes to marriage, you only have to get it right *once*. You can fail a thousand times before and it doesn't matter, because you still win. In fact, the only way to lose is to quit or never try at all, so keep reminding yourself that the odds are always in your favor.

However, if you are troubled by why a specific man walked away, consider this. First, you must accept that you do not actually know why he walked away. You don't have all the facts, so you cannot say for sure. Assuming he walked away because of how you looked or because you said the wrong thing would be a logical error. The actual reason could just as easily have been that he simply wasn't ready to give up his harem and commit to a single person.

My point is that you can determine nothing from a single episode because you don't have enough data. Agonizing over why he walked away or failed to take your bait is pointless and a waste of time. You must mentally reject that line of thought and consciously choose to replace it with the logical thought that you don't really know, so you can let it go. This process is a mental skill that will seem awkward at first, but if you keep practicing it, you will get better and better until you start doing it automatically without any effort.

However, if you keep struggling with this or can't seem to get started at all, you have two options. Start with reading the book *Feeling Good* by David Burns, MD (almost every used-book store has at least one copy for sale). It will teach you all the required mental techniques so all you have to do is practice them. However, if you are struggling to apply the techniques, you can always start going to a psychotherapist who specializes in cognitive behavioral therapy (CBT). Again, check out Appendix 2 at the end of the book on how to find a therapist who does CBT.

That said, if five different Film Directors have walked away without so much as testing your hook, you need to reexamine your game plan. Do you need to hit the gym more? Did you dress to accent your fitness? Were they the right age for you? Did you knowledgeably engage them? If everything seems to be in place, you may have just hit a run of bad luck. Don't worry, everyone has the occasional slump. It's no big deal. Just take a short break if you need to, but then get right back up on the horse and don't let your short-break turn into a long-term vacation.

If you get to 10 in a row who walk away, then it is time to up your game. Join a fitness competition to force yourself to get into awesome shape. Try changing your hairstyle to something even more stylish. You may even consider changing your hair color to something more interesting, like blond or red. Just make sure the color works for you. Upgrade your wardrobe so you look so strong and sexy that you would ask yourself for a date.

Put some time into learning how to understand and appreciate great art and music. There are some websites that will help you with this, or you can purchase an online course through sources such as Udemy or the Teaching Company. You can even take a massive open online course (MOOC) for free. Plan a trip or two to cities with great museums and other creative offerings. You never know — you might meet your Film Director, but if you don't, you'll still see some great art.

If you live in a smaller city that lacks a great art scene, take a look at the single men in your community who may be feminine leaders who have engaged the nurturing aspect of their feminine nature instead of the creative. He may be a minister for a local church or a school principal or even a Boy Scout troop leader. Physicians and psychotherapists can fall in this category, too. Get to know them and see if there is enough of a spark for them to pursue you.

Ultimately, though, the key is persistence. It may take a couple of years to find him. I will say that if you live in a medium-size city and you haven't found him after a couple of years (or less for a small city), you may have to move. Film Directors tend to cluster in cities that embrace creativity and have thriving art scenes. New York and Los Angeles, of course, top this list, but there are others on it, too, such as San Francisco, Seattle, Portland, Boston, Chicago, Philadelphia, and New Orleans.

There are also some small cities with great art scenes that you may not be aware of, such as Boulder, Colorado; Austin, Texas; Athens, Georgia; Asheville, North Carolina; and Rochester, New York. The key to small cities having great art scenes is usually the presence of a university or college, but there are exceptions such as Santa Fe, New Mexico, and Sedona, Arizona, which thrive as resort and vacation destinations for the wealthy who also love art.

Don't limit your list to these few places, since there are new, up-and-coming places joining the list all the time. Just make sure you can earn a decent living there and you actually want to live there. Check out the single scene first, because in some places, getting married is the exception rather than the rule.

However, before you pack up and move, you need to get some honest feedback, such as from your buddy who is working through this book with you, because there may be a way to tweak your game that will make all the difference and save you the trouble of moving.

You also need to give online dating a solid try before moving. I know I said earlier that you won't find your Film Director online, but moving is a big deal, so you need to exhaust every option before you take such a leap. Just be sure to look for nurturing men and not only the creative ones. Search for men in nearby towns and communities as well, not just in your immediate community.

Some singles in small towns turn a nearby city into their weekend home for dating and social reasons. You just need a good friend there who will let you crash on their couch almost every weekend so you can attend all the cool social events. This will obviously take some effort, but it is a lot easier than moving to a new city and completely starting over.

Best 5 Places to Meet a Film Director

Let's countdown the list of the five best places to meet a Film Director.

5) Open mic night or poetry slam (go regularly so you get to know everyone involved)

4) Independent or local theater show openings (volunteer so you can meet everyone who attends regularly)

3) Museum and charity galas and fund-raising events (again, volunteer)

2) Art galleries and museum openings for other artists — he'll be the one studying the art or huddled with the artist discussing their creative process while his arm-candy looks bored out of her mind

1) The opening for his art show, new film, or record release party — he'll be at the center of the group, holding court

Now that you know how and where to find your Film Director (and avoid his shadow, the Rock Star), let's take the next step. Skip to Chapter 11 to learn how to energetically manifest the Film Director meant for you.

CHAPTER TEN

The Artist

*T*he last relational archetype is the feminine supporter that I refer to as the Artist. He is similar to the Film Director in that he is creative and nurturing, but instead of organizing others, he prefers working alone or as a member of a group rather than as its leader. While he may literally be an artist or writer, he may also be a member of a band or symphony, or an architect. He may also be in a helping (nurturing) profession, such as a social worker, counselor, psychologist, schoolteacher, pediatrician, or even a psychiatrist.

He finds fulfillment by helping and nurturing others. He can be a hard worker once he is given a direction, but he may seem to lack a clear plan for his life beyond a vague dream of "making it big" in his field, despite being intelligent and skilled. On the personal level, he may be shy and soft-spoken and struggle with anxiety a bit.

When you meet him, you may be intrigued by his potential and the possibilities. He will feel like a fine lump of clay you can mold into something remarkable. However, what might throw you off is his lack of direction. He may be motivated to work on his creative projects, but he won't have a clear plan for how to make money with them. As a masculine leader, you can provide the direction necessary to make him successful and protect him from those who will try to take advantage of him.

Alternatively, you may be the one with a high-powered career who appreciates how he supports and encourages you. He will pick up the slack at home so you can put in extra time at work. A wonderful film that explores this type of non-traditional relationship is "Margaret Thatcher," starring Meryl Streep. Even though Margaret Thatcher was prime minister of England for over a decade and helped lead the free world during the Cold War, the movie focuses on her relationship with her husband, who raised their children and was her most trusted advisor.

To see how this type of relationship works in the modern world, I'll tell you about a successful couple I know with this type of non-traditional marriage. Melanie and George are a beautiful couple and they look like models. She is vivacious and outgoing, while he is reserved and gentle. She has multiple advanced degrees and has held leadership positions in professional organizations despite only being in her 20s. George, on the other hand, was an organic farmer before they got married. She currently works multiple jobs while he stays home to raise their children, which allows him to garden and cook amazing meals from the foods he grows.

The Ultimate Artist

Here is a sample profile of an Artist to help create an image in your mind's eye, so you will know him when you see him:

- **Age**: 5 years older to 15 years younger than you
- **Grooming**: hair a bit long and tousled, scruffy facial hair
- **Height**: same as yours to quite tall
- **Build**: naturally thin and lean
- **Clothing**: doesn't matter, because he makes jeans and a white T-shirt look good
- **Accessories**: understated, because any items will have personal meaning and not be for show
- **Hats**: mainly for functional reasons like a baseball cap to cover up his messy bed head
- **Shoes**: simple and comfortable, probably funky Converse high tops if he's not at work

- **Hobbies**: just his creative projects and going to see live bands you've never heard of
- **Music**: a music junky who's into a large number of little-known bands
- **Drink**: not much of a drinker, but Champagne is his favorite by far.
- **Smoke**: may smoke a cigarette here and there or vape, but is trying to quit (and you can help him with that)
- **Movies**: eclectic tastes, loves indie and art house movies
- **Sex**: hesitant and unsure of himself, so you will need to teach him
- **Actors who are Artists**: Jared Leto, Orlando Bloom, and Daniel Radcliffe.

The MAW

Now let's talk for a moment about the shadowy, dark side of the feminine supporter archetype, the MAW (Model-Musician/Actor/Whatever). He will look and energetically feel the same (because he is a feminine supporter), but he is different in a few critical ways that make him a poor choice for a husband.

One day he wants to be a musician and the next a model, and the next an artist and then an actor, and so forth. He floats from field to field and project to project without ever finishing anything. He may look like a supporter, but he's actually just lazy.

You may also get the feeling that he doesn't need a leader as much as a mommy to take care of him. If you stay long enough, you will see him for what he truly is: a parasite who lives off of others and sucks them dry before moving on to a new victim. Don't be fooled by his grand dreams and take a hard look at what he has actually accomplished.

The tricky part is that creativity is a non-linear process and can require lots of time to incubate, but genuine Artists work at their creative process diligently and regularly. Real Artists also support themselves, even if that means waiting tables or tending bar. Living on someone else's couch is a major red flag.

The other problem with a MAW is that he can be into his feelings so much that his feeling control and overwhelm him. MAWs may drink and use drugs to cope with life or use their problems and misfortunes to gain attention and sympathy from others, rather than seeking advice or support to solve them. A big clue is if you feel like you should charge him for being his therapist after spending time together. You may notice that while he seems to appreciate your advice, he never actually follows it. He continues to have the same problems over and over again that would have been easily avoided if he just listened to you.

Alternatively, the MAW is so into his creative process that he saves most of his feelings for his creativity and has little left over for you. A good example of this occurs in the 1996 Tom Hanks film "That Thing You Do," where Liv Tyler's character complains that her boyfriend, the leader of the one-hit band the film is about, saves all his feelings for his music writing and shares almost nothing with her. His emotional withholding is further compounded when he gets upset over Liv being introduced as his fiancée.

However, a MAW's greatest trap is his potential. Almost every man has potential, but a significant portion of men never live up to it. They don't consistently put in the energy and effort necessary to achieve what they are capable of doing. There are a variety of reasons, from fear of failure (and fear of success) to preferring comfort and entertainment, but in the end, the reason doesn't matter. What matters is their lack of motivation and effort.

To distinguish between the MAW and an Artist, you must ignore his potential and instead focus on his determination and persistence. The Artist has the persistence to be great, while the MAW doesn't. Instead, the MAW uses his potential like bait to hook people into supporting him, either finically or emotionally (or both), instead of using it for its intended purpose.

If you are still not sure whether you have a MAW or an Artist, look at his maturity. By maturity, I mean self-discipline, as in the ability to control impulses and resist temptation. (Yes, we are revisiting the marshmallow test here.) Does he taking care of his health by exercising, eating a healthy diet, and avoiding drugs and limiting his alcohol? Is he living within his means and maintaining a decent credit score? Is he working on his career or the necessary education for his career? Finally, do you trust him enough to start a business with him? If you can answer yes to all four questions, then he's an Artist.

I have one last warning when it comes to Artists and MAWs: Watch out for signs that he might still be in the closet or that he's not comfortable with his gender. If you find any hint that he's into gay porn, sneaks hormone pills, or is trying on women's clothing, do not ignore it.

Attracting Your Artist

Where do you find an Artist? You will have to seek him out, mostly through friends, activities, and networking, because he may not be online. He's also more likely to go to a coffee shop to work on his latest project than to a bar. The only way he will be at a bar (if he's not working there) is to hear some indie band you've never heard of, and then he will be hiding in the corner.

The good news is that when you spot him, you are free to pursue him aggressively, no holds barred. Even if you meet him online, feel free to message him first. Just approach with confidence and compliment him on something he's doing or wearing.

My only caution is to not come on too strong, because he may feel smothered and try to run. Much like how masculine men have to play it a little cool while pursuing feminine women, you need to play it a little cool with your feminine supporter Artist as well. Yes, you should ask him out and plan fabulous dates for him, but don't act as if you're that into him, even if you have sex early on. (There is no rule for you about waiting to have sex, beyond the caution about coming on too strong or if you know you fall hard and fast when you have sex.)

Artists and feminine supportive women are much like cats in this regard. Have you ever noticed that when a group of people comes into a cat's home, the cat avoids the people who try too hard to get the cat to come to them? Instead, the cat either goes to the person who hates cats or the person who allows the cat to approach, but doesn't focus their attention on the cat.

Such people often just put a hand out for the cat to smell it and rub up against it while they focus on the group. The cat is drawn to their calm confidence and patience at letting it decide how fast the relationship should advance. Next thing you know, the cat is in their lap, purring.

Similarly, you have to show some interest in your Artist, but only a hair more than the interest he shows in you. You have to read him to tell whether he is ready to move forward. Even though you are pursuing him in terms of initiating and planning activities, you still need to modulate your interest and draw him to you by generating attraction. You do this by showing him how much fun and adventure he will have if he lets you lead him.

Even though you are taking him on amazing dates, you still have to act a bit indifferent, as if you have other options and could shower all the fun and adventure on someone else if he takes too long to decide.

The reason why you need to seem a bit indifferent is because his biggest fear at this stage is that you will dominate and control him, not that he will fall too hard for you and cause you to abandon him. That slight indifference shows that you have other important goals and he is not your top priority.

It also lets him know that he will have to earn your attention and leadership. An Artist can be notoriously indecisive about being in a committed relationship. However, your slight indifference combined with your limited interest in him lets him know that while you are open to a relationship now, he is on the clock and you may move on at any moment.

Let me give you an example of how this works. Patricia was one of my students who was in a long-term half-hearted relationship with Dave. Dave is both a feminine supporter and an actual artist. Patricia was obsessed with Dave while Dave was ambivalent. Dave would frequently "take space" from Patricia, often to date other women, and wouldn't even call Patricia his girlfriend when they were together.

When they were "on" again, I would rarely hear from Patricia, but when Dave was taking space, I would hear from her quite a bit, mostly in the form of whining about Dave. As we worked together, I kept telling her to stop focusing on Dave and to focus on her own goals and interests. I also told her to refuse to be with Dave unless he committed to a constant, long-term relationship.

Patricia didn't like my advice and even stopped working with me, but I later learned that she eventually took my advice and broke off all contact with Dave. Instead, she joined a blues band to keep herself busy so she wouldn't think about Dave so much. It only took a few months before

Dave came crawling back and asked Patricia for a long-term, exclusive relationship.

As I write this, Patricia and Dave are still together without taking any breaks or any back-and-forth and are quite happy together. Not only that, Patricia's band is doing great. Her band has released its first album and stays booked for gigs, which makes Patricia very happy.

Appearance

You didn't seriously think you were going to get off the hook here, did you? Obviously, I believe in long-term health and that fitness is an important part of good health. Besides, being fit is sexy, independent from your plumbing, so get in the gym and get buff already. You can also download my dieting and exercise guide from my website (www.scottcarrollmd.com) to help you get there.

When you go out, you don't have to wear a skirt, but you still need to wear female clothing and not just show up in a suit and tie. Instead, think tight pants and sleeveless tops. Heels are fine, too, but if you really want to get his juices flowing, think dominatrix as in black leather. He may not be into S&M or B&D ... yet, but don't be surprised if he ends up liking being tied up and dominated.

As for your hair, go with short and stylish as long as it's easy to take care of. Makeup is fine, especially dark red lipstick (red is aggressive and confident), just don't turn your face into a freak show. If you are a bit pasty and don't know how to put on makeup, go to the cosmetics section of a department store and let them teach you. Just be careful with how much you spend, because this can get pricy real fast.

The most important thing is a nice smile, so if you have bad teeth, at least get them whitened. If they still look bad or are really crooked, you may have to see a dentist or orthodontist. I know that can get expensive, but there is a reason why everyone on TV has gorgeous white teeth.

Dealing With Rejection

Since you will be putting yourself out there by initiating contact and pursuing guys, you will get rejected — probably several times — before you land your man. You can whine and cuss all you want about why you have to initiate and put yourself out there all the time and why can't he do some of it, but it doesn't change the fact that it is not in your Artist's nature to initiate contact and pursue you.

Welcome to the world masculine men live in. Like masculine men, you have two choices: You can wait for him to approach you or you can make it happen yourself. I'm not saying there is zero chance he will approach you — after all, someone wins the lottery — but the odds are about the same. Just as in sales, you get a lot of no's for every yes, so one yes for every 10 no's is actually pretty good.

However, if you get really torqued by rejection, there are some things you can do about it. First, you must accept that you do not actually know why he rejected you. You don't have all the facts, so you cannot say why for sure, so to assume that he didn't like the way you looked would be a logical error. He could have been in a relationship, for all you know.

My point is that you can determine nothing from a few rejections because you don't have enough data. Agonizing over it is pointless and a waste of time. You must mentally reject that line of thought and consciously choose to replace it with the logical thought that you don't really know. Then you can let it go. This process is a mental skill that will seem awkward at first, but if you keep practicing it, you will get better and better until you start doing it automatically, without effort.

However, if you keep struggling with this or can't seem to get started at all, you have two options. You can buy and read the book Feeling Good by David Burns, MD, or you can start going to a psychotherapist who specializes in doing Cognitive Behavioral Therapy (CBT). I recommend giving the book a try first, because even if the book doesn't work, it will prime you to make faster progress with the therapist. The book is also much cheaper than therapy. You can pick up a copy at almost any used-book store or online for just a few dollars. You can also check out Appendix 2 at the end of the book to help you find a therapist if you go that route.

That said, if you are literally striking out dozens and dozens of times, something is probably wrong. Run over your procedure list in your mind to see if you are doing everything you should be doing: are in shape, dressed to show off your fit body, wore makeup that works with your look, approached likely Artists, were confident, and complimented them? If you think you did everything right, then you may not be able to see what the problem is and will need outside feedback.

This is a great time to check with the buddy who is going through the book with you. If she hasn't been your wingman yet, take her out with you so she can observe what you are doing and see which men you are approaching. Just be prepared for her to tell you exactly what you don't want to hear. We generally know what's wrong on at least a subconscious level and just can't accept the answer, usually because the answer is threatening in some way.

This is a great time to commit yourself to the truth, no matter how much the truth hurts. Be prepared for her to tell you exactly what you don't want to hear. Again, unconsciously, you already know the answer, but it threatens you emotionally in some way, which is why you didn't think of it on your own. She will tell you that your outfits suck or your makeup is wrong. Of course, the most painful, but true, advice she may give is that you need to get into better shape or stop going for guys who are too young for you.

You may be angry and ticked off at first, but understand that if there was no truth whatsoever to what she said, you would merely be puzzled about why she said that. Your strong emotional reaction is proof that she is at least partially right.

You now have the choice to swallow the bitter pill that will allow you to do something about it or keep lying to yourself and then living with the natural consequences of your choice. Ultimately, it is your choice. It always has been and always will be your choice.

While I previously said that he is probably not doing online dating, that doesn't mean that he couldn't be online. He'll just be on a free/cheap website like Plenty of Fish. Similarly, he won't pay for a dating/matchmaking service, either, because he saves his money to fund his creative projects. If you want maximize your odds of attracting your Artist by looking for him online, check out my free ebook, Attracting Your Artist Online, on my website, www.scottcarrollmd.com.

Top Five Places to Meet an Artist

Let's count down the top five places to meet an artist:

5) Local coffee shop (he'll be the guy with so much stuff that he looks like he lives there)
4) Yoga class (he'll actually be doing yoga, not just ogling the other women)
3) A live show for an eclectic, indie band (hit the same venues frequently since he's a regular)
2) Multi-artist gallery opening (he'll be hanging out by himself near his couple of pieces)
1) The launch party for his band's new album (he'll be the keyboard player hiding in the corner)

Now that you know how and where to attract your Artist (and avoid his shadow, the MAW), let's take the next step to supercharge your ability to attract him, by teaching you how to induce the universe to bring him to you. Skip to Chapter 11 to learn how to energetically manifest him.

STEP IV

Marrying Science and Spirituality

CHAPTER ELEVEN

Engaging Spirit

*E*verything we have done so far has focused on the scientific and technical aspects of attracting a quality man who will complement you well, but to attract the man you are meant for, we will have rely on the infinite intelligence of Spirit, the All That Is. As I said in the introduction, science will get you into the right ballpark, but only through the assistance of Spirit can we achieve a perfect pairing.

However, you don't need to finish this chapter (or section) before you start using everything in the preceding chapters to attract your perfect complement. After all, Spirit may already have him speeding his way to you. Until he does show up, though, keep using these spiritual and energetic techniques to manifest him and the marriage of your dreams.

If you are a dyed-in-the-wool atheist and can't wrap your head around this "mumbo-jumbo" spiritual stuff, skip ahead to Chapter 15, Getting Him to the Altar. Spirit doesn't need you to believe in it to bring you perfect gifts or to work for your highest good.

The first step to manifest the perfect man for you is to become clear about the fact that Spirit loves you and wants to bring you happiness and joy. However, there is one thing Spirit wants for you even more than your happiness and joy, and that is your emotional and spiritual growth.

Spirit's ultimate goal for your emotional and spiritual growth is for you to be a living expression of its love and kindness in this world. That doesn't mean you need to run off and become a missionary or a monk though. Spirit calls most of us to be ordinary people who work, marry, and raise families.

What this means for us is that we must embrace our growth or we may tempt Spirit to send us a difficult relationship or marriage to force us to grow. The key to embracing our spiritual and emotional growth is to learn to communicate with Spirit — real two-way conversation, not just talking to Spirit.

Communicating with Spirit

Most of us are able to talk to Spirit — that is the easy part. The hard part is learning how to listen and hear Spirit's response. Of course, our first mistake is not to even try to listen at all. Even when you try to listen, it takes regular practice to begin to hear the small and soft voice of Spirit.

The best way to practice hearing Spirit is to take time to meditate or pray for 15 minutes every morning and evening. When you meditate, start by saying what you need to say to Spirit to clear your mind to listen better. Then spend at least 10 minutes in silence, just listening. It will seem awkward at first and your mind will wander, but gently bring it back to the silence when you notice you are thinking about something else.

In the beginning, the silence may feel deafening and your mind will take every opportunity to run off to something else, but it will get easier with practice and repetition. You may get discouraged and think Spirit would never bother to communicate with you or that you don't deserve its attention, but have faith, because Spirit communicates with everyone, all the time. It just seems as if it doesn't because we continually distract ourselves and so rarely listen.

Notice I that said "communicate" and not "speak." That is because words are the least reliable way to communicate. Words are the most open to misinterpretation and confusion. Rather, Spirit's first choice is to use feelings. Feelings are the most clear and least confusing. They also contain our deepest truth.

If you ever want to know your deepest truth, seek out your deepest feelings. Pay attention to the feelings that come up while you sit in the silence, especially in relation to the thoughts and situations that arise in your mind. As the feelings come up, stay with them to give them the time to change and evolve over several minutes.

Feelings are like bubbles exhaled by a deep-sea diver that slowly rise to the surface and, just like the deepest bubbles, the deepest feelings take the longest to surface in your consciousness. You cannot rush them. You can only give them the time necessary to make the long journey up and then calm the waters of your mind so you can perceive them when they do finally surface.

As you pay attention and get better at being aware of your deepest feelings, you will start to notice that your feelings have different qualities and come from different places. Initially, your feelings may seem angry or fearful. These initial feelings come from all of the negative emotions we don't want to feel and have pushed down into our unconsciousness.

These angry and fearful feelings usually show up first, but if you stay with the silence, you will start to notice that underneath the negative feelings of fear and anger are more positive feelings — feelings of love and joy. Pay attention to these positive feelings because they are your deepest truth and are from Spirit. You will know this because they will always be loving and joyful and feel as if they come from someplace other than yourself, a wiser and kinder place.

As you get more skilled at perceiving these deep feelings of love and joy when you meditate, you will start to have thoughts and even experiences that seem to come from the same place as the deep positive feelings. You will be able to recognize these thoughts and experiences as being from Spirit because they embody love and joy at their core.

After awhile, you will start to have these feelings and thoughts when you are engaged in simple, mindless tasks like washing the dishes, taking a shower, or walking someplace, not just when you are meditating. You may also notice that the words of a song or something a friend said in passing, or even a fortune cookie, will seem to perfectly answer one of your questions or encourage you to do something. It may seem crazy, but this is how Spirit communicates.

Once the lines of communication with Spirit are open, you will start to get messages about what you need to do to prepare yourself to receive Spirit's gift — the perfect relationship it is preparing for you. Heed these messages, because following them may be critical for Spirit to be able to send him to you and for you to be prepared and able to receive and accept him into your life.

Forgiveness and Blessings

Forgiveness is a common theme in these messages. You may be guided to forgive your ex who mistreated or harmed you. You may need to let go of the anger in your heart so your heart can be filled with love for someone else. Notice that this forgiveness is of the heart and not the mind. Forgiving and letting go of your anger does not mean you must forget or give your ex another chance to mistreat you.

You may also be guided to forgive your parents for all the things they have done to harm you, and for their shortcomings as both people and parents. Similarly, this is forgiveness of the heart and not the mind. You will just be letting go of your anger, not giving them the opportunity to keep harming or mistreating you.

Finally, you will be guided to lovingly forgive yourself. Maybe you still feel guilty over a past relationship or getting a divorce. Maybe you cheated or mistreated someone. Maybe you were bad with your money and had to declare bankruptcy. Whatever it was, it is okay to forgive yourself.

Please accept that there is no purpose in continuing to feel guilty and refusing to forgive yourself. Your stubbornness and desire to keep punishing yourself is what blocks you from receiving Spirit's gifts and blessings. That is because Spirit will never force its gifts upon us. Spirit's love is so infinite and complete that it would never take away our free will, even if it were our will to endure excruciating and needless suffering.

Forgiving yourself is how you let go of your need to punish yourself for past mistakes and open yourself to receiving every gift Spirit longs to give you. As part of forgiving yourself, you may be led to make amends. Notice that making amends is not the same as continuing to punish yourself. Making amends is actually about doing what is loving and possible to heal the people you've harmed and righting past mistakes.

One key difference between making amends and continuing to punish yourself is that making amends is circumscribed and limited, while punishment is open-ended and ongoing. Making amends also either actually helps the person you harmed or, if that is not possible, pays it forward by increasing the love and compassion on our tiny planet.

As you forgive yourself and everyone who has hurt you, you may also feel guided to start blessing them. You may be led to start asking for Spirit to bring whatever healing they need into their lives and to bless them with the perfect gifts that will bring them the same love and joy you seek.

Hidden Gifts, Gratitude, and Letting Go

As you forgive and bless yourself and everyone in your life, you may start to notice gifts hidden in your past traumas and mistakes. For example, if someone was mistreating you, that situation enabled you to learn how to recognize and stop the mistreatment, so you now have the ability to prevent others from mistreating you. Maybe you are able to see that something you wanted was not aligned with your highest good or that something you do in relationships just doesn't work.

As you start to see these hidden gifts, you will begin to notice that you have received so many gifts and valuable experiences that you will no longer see your past relationships as failures, but rather as successive experiences that have helped you become the amazing person you are.

As you do, your anger, grief, and disappointment with your life will turn into gratitude for all the gifts you have been given, because you will see as Spirit sees. Spirit sees nothing as truly good or bad, but rather as that which does or does not serve you. Even then, Spirit knows that most things that seem not to serve us only appear that way because we are too close to them in terms of time and perspective. You may have noticed that when you look back on some tragedy or loss that occurred years earlier, the event changed you in some beneficial way or altered your path, leading to a greater journey and grander destination.

From this place of deep gratitude, you may feel the need to change certain things in your life — a spring cleaning if you will — because you will need to let go of whatever you are holding onto to free up space to receive new gifts from Spirit.

For example, you may need to stop hooking up with your ex or that hot guy at the gym. Maybe you need to finalize your divorce or stop seeing all men as cheaters or abusers. Whatever it is, once you have let it go or taken care of it, you are finally ready to ask for and receive Spirit's perfect relationship for you.

Similar to Spirit's forgiveness preceding your request for forgiveness, Spirit's gifts are already on their way to you even before you ask. In fact, you don't even need to ask. Merely expressing gratitude is sufficient because Spirit's gifts are already on their way to you.

When Forgiveness and Gratitude Aren't Working

You might be thinking "Baloney" about now because in your experience, Spirit's gifts are few and far between. There are a few reasons why your experience feels different. First, just as Spirit communicates with everyone all the time while few listen, Spirit gives gifts all the time, but few of us allow ourselves to receive them.

Even when we receive them, we often don't see them as perfect gifts, but rather as problems or challenges. We also don't recognize Spirit's gifts because they don't show up in the precise form we imagined, such as with abs of steel and a six-figure salary.

The second reason Spirit's gifts don't seem to show up despite our being ready and open has to do with our free will and the fact that we ask for things from different parts of ourselves. The problem is that our heart wants one thing, our mind wants something else, and our soul wants something completely different. Their desires also are often incompatible or even contradictory.

What can Spirit do? If Spirit grants your heart's desire, it is taking free will away from your mind and soul by forcing something on them. If Spirit grants your soul's desire instead, it is forcing something on your heart and mind. Since the one thing Spirit will never do is take away our free will, Spirit waits for us to get clear within ourselves. Once we align the desires of our heart, mind, and soul, Spirit is then free to bless us without limit or measure.

Aligning Your Heart and Mind

We usually know what our mind wants because our mind expresses itself in our conscious thoughts. A little bit of self-reflection and quiet contemplation is usually enough to get a clear picture of your mind's desires.

Becoming aware of our heart's desires takes a little more effort, but still isn't all that difficult. We just need to become aware of our feelings, especially the deeper ones that are below the surface of our consciousness. Just as I described earlier in this chapter, we have to quiet the mind to let our deeper feelings bubble up.

It is not unusual to have a conflict between the heart and the mind. For example, our mind wants a loving marriage while our heart is actually fearful and associates marriage with being limited or controlled, or even with being abused. However, because our mind wants to be married so badly, it judges our heart's fears as childish and foolish and represses them.

The solution is to resist judging your heart and to see your heart's feelings as valid or simply true for your heart, even if they are not true for your mind. Once you do that, you can then have a dialogue between your heart and mind. Oftentimes, if the mind can simply accept what the heart feels, then the heart is satisfied. Other times, the heart can be satisfied if the mind can reassure it that the mind will defend the heart from whatever it fears.

A good technique for facilitating a dialogue between the heart and mind is to have a written conversation using the two sides of the body to represent these two parts of ourselves. Take a piece of paper and draw a line from top to bottom, dividing the paper in half and use your dominant hand to write down the mind's question. On the opposite side of the page, use your non-dominant hand to write down the heart's response. Yes, the heart's response will look like a kindergartner wrote it, but that is good because you are tapping into the pre-logical phase of your life where your thoughts and feelings were the same.

Occasionally, validation and reassurance are insufficient and the mind may have to let go of what it wants. This is not as hard as it sounds, because happiness is a feeling and thus governed by the heart. Ultimately, how can you be happy if your heart is not happy?

If you mind is unable to surrender to your heart, then it is time to get professional help in the form of psychodynamic psychotherapy. Avoid cognitive behavioral therapy (CBT) and other "mind–oriented" therapies because they work by using logic and thought to override or correct the emotions. CBT is highly effective for treating irrational anxieties, but it is counterproductive for resolving conflicts between the heart and mind as we are trying to do here. See Appendix 2 for guidance on finding a psychodynamic psychotherapist.

Psychodynamic psychotherapy can seem unfocused and slow, but be patient, because it is making changes deep below the surface that take time to become visible. Just use the dominant/non-dominant writing technique to keep track of your progress.

Aligning Your Heart and Mind with Your Soul

While you are working on getting your heart and mind in synch, you also need to get clear on what your soul desires. Listening to your soul is similar to listening to Spirit, and you can use the same meditation techniques I described earlier in this chapter.

Remember, your soul is much more directly connected to Spirit than your heart or mind, so you can ask for Spirit's assistance in this process. Listening involves sitting in the silence and allowing those deep feelings of love and joy to bubble up. Notice that your soul primarily uses feelings to communicate with you for the same reason Spirit does.

If you have been able to follow my earlier instructions to allow Spirit to communicate with you, you may have trouble distinguishing between a message from Spirit and one from your soul. Often, the message is the same, so you don't have to distinguish between the two, but if the messages are different you'll have to resolve the question.

Some messages tend to be more personal and specific to you. They may give you specific instructions, directions, or answers. Other messages may seem less specific to your question or situation and may contain general answers like "have faith" or "patience" or even "It doesn't really matter". Such general messages tend come from Spirit while the more specific ones are from your soul.

Another way to tell if a message is from Spirit or your soul is by its tone. Messages from your soul can seem more focused and even insistent while Spirit sounds soft and gentle like a whisper.

If you still can't distinguish where the message is coming from, ask Spirit to help you understand and be clear. If sincerely asked, Spirit will provide you with clarity. Spirit has the entire universe at its disposal so the possibilities are endless, but often Spirit will simply be silent so only your soul is communicating with you.

Once you are clear on where a message is from, you still have to choose which message to follow. You are always free to choose either, but Spirit tends to be less concerned than your soul about whether or not you follow its advice. Your soul isn't a tyrant however, always demanding its own way. Much like Spirit, it will not force you to do what it wants, but over the years, I've come to see that ignoring your soul's desires doesn't tend to work out in the long run.

While sometimes your soul will relent and accept what the heart and mind want, especially when your heart and mind stand firm together, I have learned that in the end, listening to your soul — even when what it wants doesn't make sense — will eventually lead you to greater joy and satisfaction than what your heart and mind wanted.

Aligning your heart and mind with your soul begins with choosing to practice radical acceptance where you suspend judgment, suspend desire and commit to following your soul. In radical acceptance, you may not see the path or even know exactly where you are heading, but instead you let go of needing to understand the process, trusting that your soul will lead you to your greatest joy.

Practicing radical acceptance for your mind is straight forward and just requires consistently choosing to follow your soul. Your heart may be another story however and require assistance from your mind. You can use the dominant/non-dominate hand dialogue technique to understand your heart's resistance. As before, validating and reassuring your heart often satisfies it, but if not your heart may be in need of healing.

Start by asking for Spirit's assistance in healing your heart. While the possibilities are endless, don't be surprised if Spirit directs you to go to psychotherapy. You will probably be guided to do psychodynamic psychotherapy, but follow Spirit's guidance if it leads you to CBT first. Certain psychological and emotional wounds are better healed by psychotherapy than by spiritual practices.

Once your heart has been healed, it can more easily surrender to your soul. You can use the dominant/non-dominant hand writing technique to track your heart's progress. Your mind can also help, just be patient and gentle with your heart like you would with a child, answering your heart's questions and reassuring it when necessary.

This process can take some time, but when your heart, mind, and soul are in agreement, life just flows as if you were swimming with the current rather than against it. Then Spirit can shower you with all the gifts and blessings it has for you since your heart, mind, and soul are in synch.

Receiving Spirit's Gifts

Now that your heart, mind, and soul desire the same thing and you are thanking Spirit daily for the perfect relationship that is speeding its way to you, you need to prepare yourself to receive that gift of a perfect relationship. You need to avoid these common mistakes that prevent so many people from receiving Spirit's perfect gifts in their lives.

One common mistake is to reject the gift because it doesn't look exactly like what we expected. Namely, we are thinking one thing, but Spirit has a different and better idea. We reject the gift because we judge it from the limited knowledge and perspective of our mind.

The mind is extremely good at seizing upon superficial factors to rule someone out, such as height, income, dress, and so forth. Instead, keep meditating and listen to Spirit and see where it directs you. Give yourself time to allow the deeper factors that are critically important for relationships to rise to the surface and reveal themselves. You may then start to glimpse what Spirit has in mind for you. Don't be surprised if it's far better than what you were thinking.

When my wife and I met in person for the first time on a coffee date, she had spent the whole day giving massages and couldn't run home to get ready because her last client had run late. She was tired and almost canceled, but something inside told her to come anyway. We had a nice conversation, but their weren't any fireworks or a lot of chemistry. We both just kind of liked the other. That was it — the loves of our lives and we just kind of liked each other.

But something deep inside of both of us gently encouraged us to give it another chance. We didn't see each other again for over a week, but the second date went well despite a lack of sparks. It wasn't until the end of the third date that the fireworks started exploding.

The point is that you don't want to be too hasty and decide someone isn't right for you just because they don't wow you right off the bat. Obviously, you don't want to ignore any red flags or signs of danger, but try to sit with it for a while and see what your soul and Spirit say.

You're probably new at this listening to your soul thing, so you need to be careful and not walk off a cliff because you thought your soul/Spirit told you to do so. Take your time and clarify what Spirit wants you to do before doing anything that doesn't make sense. Always remember that you may have misunderstood the message, especially if it seems wrong or dangerous.

If you just can't stop your mind from judging everyone and everything (remember, there is a difference between awareness and judgment), you may need to go to therapy to move past it. Some of us were raised with so much judgment and criticism that it has become a part of us and we have trouble letting go, even when it is not really ours and came from a critical parent or partner.

Both psychodynamic and cognitive behavioral (CBT) therapy are effective for this and will increase your happiness, because we usually judge and criticize ourselves more harshly than anyone else. Unrestrained judgment and criticism is also a great way to ruin a marriage (and your children).

The last common mistake is that we think Spirit works on our time frame. One of the hardest answers to hear from Spirit is "patience my beloved child." We naturally want our gifts to arrive immediately. However, Spirit sees all things and knows when we are truly ready. Sometimes the heart needs more time to heal even though we may feel ready now. Trust that Spirit knows the perfect time for everything to happen and remember that a field needs to lie fallow for it to grow good crops.

In Review

- Meditate (or pray) for 15 minutes every morning and evening to learn to listen to Spirit.
- Forgive yourself and everyone who has harmed you to let go of the anger and fear that blocks you from receiving Spirit's gifts.

- Bless yourself and everyone who has harmed you by calling on Spirit to heal them and bless them with the same love and joy you seek.
- Be open to the possibility of gifts being hidden in your losses, tragedies, and failures.
- Align the desires of your heart, mind, and soul to enable Spirit to give you its greatest gifts.
- Use the dominant/non-dominant handwriting technique to align your heart and mind.
- Choosing to surrender to your soul's desires leads to your greatest joy.
- Ask Spirit for assistance in helping your heart surrender to your soul, it may even send you to psychotherapy.
- Resist judging Spirit's gifts if they don't show up in the precise form we expect.
- Accept that Spirit works on its own timeframe and knows when we are ready to its gifts.

CHAPTER TWELVE

Aligning Yourself

*I*n the previous chapter, we worked on creating the spiritual foundation necessary for manifesting your perfect complement (Athlete, Engineer, Film Director, or Artist) by learning to listen to Spirit; aligning your heart, mind, and soul; and clearing the barriers to receiving Spirit's gifts. Now we will expand on that foundation by teaching you to align yourself with the subtle energies that constantly flow around and through us, and then teach you how use the subtle energies to manifest your perfect complement most efficiently.

The Subtle Energies

The subtle energies I'm talking about are spiritual energies, not literal physical energies such as light or heat, and they cannot be detected by standard scientific methods. Many indigenous cultures around the world recognize the existence of these spiritual energies. In India, these energies are called "prana"; in China, they are called "chi." Among the indigenous peoples of the Andes mountain range of South America, they are known as "sami" (light energy) and "hucha" (dark/heavy energy).

These subtle energies flow through us via our chakras (spinning energetic vortexes that literally anchor the soul to the body) and connect us to all other living beings and even events and places. They also form patterns that act like energetic blueprints from which all things and events are created. These energetic patterns are so critical that nothing exists without first existing as an energetic pattern, including relationships.

When you align yourself with these subtle energies, you can then influence and move them to create the energetic patterns you want, which the universe then automatically manifests in physical reality. Yes, you can just rely on everything you learned in the previous chapter about aligning, listening, and removing blocks (and you need to do those things first to be able to directly engage the energetic patterns), but working directly with the energetic patterns supercharges the process.

If you are having trouble embracing this approach because of your religious beliefs, I would encourage you to give it a chance. To the best of my knowledge, these techniques do not violate any religious belief and you can think of them as simply different forms of prayer. In fact, prayer works because it is able to engage and influence the subtle energy flows. It's just that the way most people pray is not the most effective method for doing this. These techniques don't violate a belief in God because I would say that God designed the universe to be sensitive to these techniques. Keep reading and see if you can use at least a few of them.

Alignment and Manifestation

The first step to all manifestation is to align yourself with the subtle energy flows around you because you cannot influence the subtle energy flows if you are not aligned with them. In fact, aligning yourself is the most challenging aspect of the manifestation process and often takes the most time and effort, but once you are aligned, manifesting whatever you want is relatively easy.

However, manifestation is not magic. You still have to do all the physical steps of building or creating something. You must still plow the field and plant the crops and go to school to earn the degree, but the process flows smoothly with relatively few bumps or obstacles (and then, as the Taoists say, you flow like a river around the boulder).

An old South American story about a powerful medicine man who was particularly adept at manifesting rain illustrates this point. In fact, he had never failed to bring rain to a village when requested. One day, a distant village asked him to come because it hadn't rained for several weeks and their crops were dying. When he arrived, he commanded that a hut be quickly built for him so he could pray. When it was finished, he went inside and didn't come out for three days.

For three days, he stayed in the hut, not even leaving for meals, but still there wasn't a cloud in the sky, much less any rain. On the third day, just as the villagers were about to pull him out and demand he make it rain, he came out and sat at the edge of the village, chanting. Less than an hour later, dark clouds rolled in over the mountains and big drops of rain began pelting the ground. The villagers were relieved, but they asked him why it took so long to make it rain.

He replied that it didn't take him three days to make it rain, but rather that it took him three days to get the village back in alignment because it was in such a state of disconnection.

As with the village, aligning yourself can be challenging, but once you do so, manifesting is then straightforward.

How can you tell if you are aligned? One fun and easy way is to see how many green lights you can catch the next time you're driving. This method works best when there are several lights on the way to wherever you are going. Of course, please stay calm, drive at a safe speed, and try to flow with the traffic. Don't try to pass people (unless they are driving dangerously or much too slowly) or weave in and out of traffic to get ahead.

Pay attention to how many green lights you hit during your trip. Anything below 50% suggests you're not aligned; 50 to 70% suggests you are somewhat aligned; and 70 to 90% is ideal. Just remember you will almost never get 100% because Spirit will still give you the occasional red light to keep you away from dangerous drivers and potential accidents.

Another area to assess whether you are aligned is to look at the flow of your day. Do people call or stop by your desk at work at just the right times? Do your efforts at work seem to be effective? Do you complete tasks efficiently? Do your relationships with friends, family, and coworkers seem to flow? Do others get what you mean easily, and do you understand them easily as well?

One of my favorite clues to let me know whether I'm aligned is when I realize I need to call someone just as the phone rings because that person is calling me. I could go on and on with examples, but the basic idea is that when you are in alignment, life is not random and nothing that happens is just a coincidence. It is like being in the "zone," where you get a lot more heads than tails and your efforts flow with little wasted energy.

Alignment vs. Harmony

Alignment with the subtle energies is not the same as being in harmony, however. Harmony implies a passive and peaceful relationship with other things, while alignment can mean you are at odds or even in conflict with something and work hard to oppose it. When the tai chi master throws his opponent across the room while barely (or not even) touching him using his chi, the tai chi master is not in harmony with his opponent, but he is in alignment with both his and his opponent's energy. When the cheetah sprints and catches the gazelle that is almost as fast, but is far more agile and has a big head start, the cheetah is not in harmony but is in alignment with both its own and the gazelle's energy.

The point is that even disharmony and open conflict can be forms of alignment in certain circumstances.

Fire-breathing

With some practice, you should start to have a sense of when you are in alignment and when you are not. As you become aware, you can then start to shift into greater degrees of alignment. One of the simplest ways to move into alignment is to start doing a type of meditation called "fire-breathing."

During fire-breathing meditation, you establish and enhance your connection to two important sources of the subtle energies: the feminine energy of the Earth and the masculine energies of the universe. Simply by establishing these two connections, you increase your alignment. The energy you draw from these two sources also can be used to increase your connection and to modify the energy flows around you by a number of methods.

Basically, fire-breathing enables you to gather the fuel that all the other energetic techniques require to work. It's also great for picking up your energy instead of reaching for coffee or a soda. Just don't do it right before bed or it can keep you awake.

Be sure to blow your nose first. Sterile nasal saline can clear the mucus from your nose and make the fire-breathing easier. Netti pots and other sinus rinsing techniques can also work, but make sure that any fluid that goes into your nose is sterile.

Sit cross-legged on the floor (or a stool, if you're too stiff, like me) and clasp your hands behind your back with your index fingers pointed down toward the earth. Keep your head up, your spine as straight as it can be, and your eyes closed. The illustration is an example:

Rearview.

Rapidly breathe in and out through your nose, using your belly to move the air, while keeping your shoulders still and your head up and spine straight.

Try to breathe for 5 minutes; at first, you'll probably only be able to go 1 to 2 minutes, maybe only 30 seconds. Push yourself a little bit, but don't give yourself an asthma attack or coughing fit.

The rapid breathing may make you feel dizzy (which is why you should never try to do it while standing). If you start to feel dizzy, stop and move to the next step with a deep inhale.

On the last fire breath, take as deep a breath as you can, then exhale fully. On the next breath, inhale in three steps with a brief pause between each phase of inhalation. You want to reach maximum inhalation with the third step and then hold your breath. (If you have poor lung function or severe breathing problems, skip to the last step where you are holding your breath and pulsing.)

While holding your breath, imagine a silver cord extending down from the bottom of your spine, all the way down to the center of the Earth. Next, repetitively tighten your pelvic floor muscles (just like a Kegel exercise) to "pump" the silver energy of the Earth up the cord into your spine. Keep pumping the silver energy up the cord with repetitive contractions every second or two until you need to take a breath.

Once you need to take a breath, stop pumping and start breathing normally. Release your hands and move your arms so they are over your head. Clasp your hands together again with your index fingers extended and pointing toward the sky. Keep your arms as straight as possible with your head up, shoulders square, and spine as straight as possible, as in the illustration.

Front view.

Begin another round of fire-breathing, by breathing in and out rapidly through your nose. Continue the fire-breathing until you get tired, feel a little dizzy, or start to become short of breath. End the fire-breathing with a large last breath that you slowly exhale from your mouth. Again, take the three-step inhalation and hold your breath.

This time, imagine a golden cord extending from the top of your head all the way to the center of the universe. Again tighten and relax your pelvic floor muscles (Kegel exercise) to pump the energy down the cord, only this time, the energy from the universe will be golden instead of silver.

Continue to hold your breath and pump the golden energy down the cord until you need to take a breath.

Once you take a breath, unclasp your hands and lower your arms down to your lap, and breathe normally for a couple of minutes. Allow the silver energy from the Earth and the golden energy from the universe to mingle and infuse your spinal column.

You have now completed one cycle of fire-breathing. What you have just done is awaken the energetic system of your body and then recharge it by feeding it a combination of the feminine energy from the Earth and the masculine energy from the universe.

Now repeat the cycle of fire-breathing two more times for a total of three cycles, calling in both feminine and masculine energy. If you are pressed for time, you can do one or two cycles, but three is ideal. Avoid doing half-cycles because you don't want to create an imbalance between the feminine and masculine energies.

When you have completed the three cycles of fire-breathing, stay in your current posture with your hands in your lap as the energy from the last cycle infuses your system. While breathing normally with your eyes closed, turn your attention to your chakras — the spinning vortexes that anchor your soul to your body.

Opening and Cleaning Your Chakras

Chakras are small spinning funnels of subtle energy that project forward a couple of inches outside our bodies. The small end of the funnel originates in our spinal column or brain, while the large end projects forward out of the body. They also spin like a clock from the perspective of someone facing you.

There are seven chakras that line up down the center of our body from the top of the head to the public bone (just above your genitalia; see the picture for details). The chakras literally anchor the soul to the body (the soul envelopes the body, not the other way around). They are also the portals through which the subtle energies flow both into and out of us, and allow us to connect to the energy patterns around us.

Front view of the seven chakras.

However, our chakras can become clogged and restricted with dark and heavy energy that builds up like sludge in a pipe and limits our ability to connect to outside energy patterns. This heavy energy is created by negative interactions with others and by simply not being in alignment with the energy flows and patterns around us. Luckily, there is a simple method for removing the heavy energy and restoring optimal flow that you can do in the shower.

While standing in the shower with the water on and your eyes closed, use your non-dominant hand to find your chakras. When your hand passes over a chakra, it may feel a little warmer or cooler than nearby areas, or you may feel a slight resistance or tingling in your hand. This may take some practice, since you are feeling for subtle differences, but if you can't find them, just imagine them being in the locations on the picture above.

The chakras are generally found in the following locations: The first chakra passes through your pubic bone, just above your genitalia. The second chakra is located just below your navel. The third chakra goes through your solar plexus (the upper part of your abdomen, just below where your ribs come together). The fourth chakra goes through your heart. The fifth chakra passes through the lower part of your neck, just above your sternum. The sixth chakra passes through your forehead, just above your eyes. The seventh chakra points up through the top of your head rather than forward.

Once you have located (or imagined) your chakras, start with your first chakra, next to your pubic bone, and unwind it by moving your hand in a counterclockwise direction, as if you're turning back the hands of a clock for others to see. As you spin the chakra backward, you may mentally perceive a dark, fog-like slime collecting on your hand.

As the slime builds up, use the water from the shower to wash the slime off your hand. Don't let the slime drip back on you; just let it fall back to Mother Earth. She lives off of this dark energy, much like a garden thrives on compost, and in exchange, she gives us the silver energy we received during fire-breathing.

You may need to spin and rinse a few times before you stop getting dark energy out of the chakra. Before continuing to the second chakra (just below your belly button), you must rewind the first chakra by spinning your hand in a clockwise direction. Always rewind a chakra before unwinding the next one, or you might start to disconnect your soul from your body, which takes extensive training to do safely.

Use the same unwinding and rinsing process with each chakra to remove any heavy or dark energy in it, being sure to rewind each chakra before unwinding the next one. As you clean out your chakras, energy will automatically flow more freely through them and bring you into alignment with the flows and patterns around you.

You may also notice that you are able to draw more silver and golden energy during fire-breathing when your chakras are clear. As you continue to fire-breathe and clean your chakras regularly, you will start to communicate more easily with Spirit when you meditate and will be able to ask Spirit questions and receive answers as if you were having a conversation. Such conversations are a clear sign that you are in a high degree of alignment.

In Review

- You must align your subtle energy flows with the energy flows and patterns around you to begin manifesting your intentions for marriage.
- Alignment is not necessarily being in harmony.
- Use daily fire-breathing meditation to energize your system and bring it into alignment.
- Clean your chakras to improve your energy flow and bring it into alignment.

CHAPTER THIRTEEN

MANIFESTING HIM

*I*f you haven't read and applied the two previous chapters (Engaging Spirit and Aligning Yourself), go back and do that now. The techniques in this chapter are unlikely to be successful if you haven't completed the preparatory work in the preceding two chapters. That is because these techniques for manifestation require that you be in alignment with the energy flows and patterns around you to influence them.

Just remember that it typically takes one to three months of consistently using the previous techniques to move into alignment so you can begin manifesting.

Now that you have engaged Spirit and moved into better degree of alignment, you are ready to energetically attract the man you are meant for. However, before you begin, I want to share some general information that will help you. In the two prior chapters, I've been fairly explicit about what to do, but manifestation is an intuitive process, so I can only give you guidelines. Of course, I will tell you if you shouldn't do something or if something is dangerous, but other than that, trust your inner sense of how to apply these techniques. Use your meditation (especially after fire-breathing) to guide you in applying them.

The Fire Ceremony

One of the simplest manifestation techniques is to use a fire ceremony (the night of a full moon tends to work best). All manifestation is based on the principle that our intentions are creative and have the potential to induce the universe to manifest our intention. However, even though we have intentions all the time, they don't typically result in manifestation for a variety of reasons.

First, we often have multiple intentions at any given time that contradict one another or are incompatible with each other and then cancel each other out (we addressed this in the chapter on engaging Spirit). Second, we are often not in alignment with the energy flows and patterns around us, so our intentions get lost and fail to resonate with the patterns and flows around us (we addressed this issue in the previous chapter). Third, our intentions aren't energetically strong and don't have enough power to induce the universe to do anything.

The purpose of the fire ceremony (and the other techniques in this chapter) is to address this third issue: lack of power. They are designed to boost the power of your intention so the universe will respond and actually manifest it.

The first step for doing a fire ceremony is to find a safe and private place to do the fire. A fire pit, grill, or fireplace will work; just make sure it is designed to burn wood or charcoal and not natural gas, for obvious reasons. If you are using someone else's property or are on public property, make sure your have permission and that you follow all safety procedure and rules. Be prepared to extinguish your fire completely if it spreads. Never leave a fire unattended.

You will need a small bottle of virgin olive oil and three small sticks. You will also need a small amount of firewood, consisting of several small and medium-sized sticks. You don't need any logs because when you are doing a fire ceremony you have to stay with the fire while it is burning and can't put it out with water until all flame is gone and only coals are left.

You need paper or leaves to get the fire started and, of course, matches or a lighter. You also need plenty of water (or dirt, if your fire is on the ground) to douse the coals completely so they are cool to the touch when you are done.

If you are in an urban area where you don't have access to an appropriate place for a fire ceremony, you can still do one symbolically with a candle and toothpicks. The candle will represent your fire and the toothpicks represent the sticks you will burn. You'll need a small metal tray or ceramic dish that won't burn or scorch, tweezers to hold the toothpicks when you burn them, and a small amount of olive oil that you won't actually burn. You will follow the same procedures as a regular fire ceremony, but I'll cue you when to make the substitutions.

On a full moon, start by finding (or being intuitively led) to a safe place for the ceremony where you won't be disturbed. Next, protect the ceremony space by asking for the protection of the four directions: South, West, North, and East, in that order. Then ask Mother Earth below you and Father Sky above you to protect your fire ceremony. If you want to make your protection even stronger, you can go to my website (www. scottcarrollmd.com) to download a script to use.

After obtaining protection, build a small fire in the safe place you've chosen or been led to. Once your fire is going, take the bottle of virgin olive oil and hold it up to honor the four directions (South, West, North, and East) for protecting your fire and ask for their assistance in manifesting your intentions. Next, honor Mother Earth below you and Father Sky above you with the bottle while asking for their assistance in manifesting your intentions. Next, place a few drops of the oil in the fire. Be careful because the oil is highly flammable and can make your fire flare up.

Once your fire calms and the flames go back down, repeat the process of honoring the directions and Mother Earth and Father Sky and anointing the fire with oil two more times, for a total of three times. You can also sing a soft lullaby to the fire to help it calm down after each dose of oil.

If you are using the candle-and-toothpick method, you will still honor the directions and Mother Earth and Father Sky and ask for their assistance, but will only pretend to pour the oil on your candle.

After your fire calms down, following the third dose of oil, take a twig (or toothpick) and blow on it three times while holding an image of whatever you are manifesting in your mind. In our case, you will hold an image that represents the man and marriage you are meant for. You may imagine being walked down the aisle or going on your honeymoon;

whatever image resonates most strongly with you. Then place the twig in the fire and let it completely burn to manifest your intention.

If you are using toothpicks and a candle, use a pair of tweezers to hold the toothpick while burning it. It's okay if you can't burn the toothpick completely. Just burn as much as you safely can and put the unburned part on the tray or dish you are using.

You will be burning three twigs or toothpicks in this manner during your fire ceremony (repeat the step above two more times). Focus all three twigs on manifesting your marriage for now, but generally, you can manifest a different thing with each twig. Be sure to stay with your fire while holding your intentions in your mind until the twigs are completely burned up and your fire is just coals without any flame.

Once your fire is just coals with no flame, you can put water on the coals so they are completely out and cool to the touch. Now you need to thank and release the four directions and Mother Earth and Father Sky, using the same order (South, West, North, East, Mother Earth, and then Father Sky). To release a direction, you just need to tell it that you are releasing it and then thank it three times for protecting your fire and helping you manifest your intention (see my website for a script to release and thank the directions).

It typically takes about 30 days for a fire ceremony to manifest your intentions. However, if your intentions haven't manifested after a few weeks, you can repeat your fire ceremony on the night of the next full moon, which will strengthen your manifestation.

You can also use the other techniques described in this chapter at the same time as the fire ceremony. If you decide to burn an offering (described below), you can do so as part of your fire ceremony. Just burn the offering after the twigs and then complete the fire ceremony by putting the coals out and releasing the directions as previously described.

Offerings

Another relatively simple technique for boosting the power of your intention so it can manifest is making an offering that is then buried or burned (often during a fire ceremony). Typically, these offerings involve wrapping up a variety of objects in paper or other burnable or biodegradable material.

Burning is the most rapid method for manifesting the offering because the intention placed in the offering is immediately released to work as the physical objects are burned. Burying also works, but it is a bit slower since it takes 30 to 40 days for the energy to be released to work while the offering decays in the ground.

You can put almost anything in an offering, but if you plan on burning it, be careful and don't put anything toxic, explosive, or excessively flammable in it. Similarly, if you plan to bury your offering, make sure you're using items that are biodegradable and safe for our delicate environment. Practically speaking, you want everything in your offering to burn or decay completely to maximize the effect. Items such as foods, wine or juice, herbs, feathers, flowers, photos, and natural fabric and materials work best.

Offerings are best made as part of an intuitive process based on your specific situation and the messages you receive through your meditation. There is no right or wrong answer about what to include (beyond the safety issue of not including anything dangerous). However, there are common offering ingredients you can use if you don't get a specific suggestion during meditation.

Some examples of items commonly used include sweets and candy to attract the "sweetness of life" (heart-shaped Valentine candy is particular good for romantic relationships) and fats such as lard or shortening to represent the "richness of life." A few drops of wine or other alcoholic spirit are also great. Various foods also work, such as grain for abundance.

Complex things you can't burn or bury can be represented by drawing a picture of them on a small piece of paper that can be placed in the offering. Afterward, you will wrap the offering up in a large sheet of paper or tortilla and tie it with a string. Pretty wrapping paper (as long as it doesn't contain metal or plastic) is great for burning, and large tortillas work great if your offering is small and you plan on burying it. Just don't use old newspaper or advertisements unless there is something specific on the newspaper or advertisement that relates to the offering.

It often helps to spend some time meditating after fire-breathing, listening for guidance on what to include in your offering and whether to bury or burn it. Next, you should gather everything you will need before you start. Begin by spreading the paper or tortilla out in front of you and then doing three rounds of fire-breathing. As you add objects, briefly close your eyes and meditate on which object to add next and to know when you are done.

Since we are manifesting your perfect marriage, your offering will probably look something like this, but follow any specific instructions you get during meditation, assuming it is safe to do so.

The first object added is the lard or shortening, which you should mould into the shape of a heart to symbolize love or a ring to symbolize a wedding ring. Next, add a picture or something to symbolize yourself. Then add a picture or something to symbolize the man you are manifesting. Next, add something to symbolize a wedding or marriage. If you want children, you can use a picture of a family here.

Next, add some sweets or candy to represent the sweetness of life (heart-shaped Valentine candy is great for our purpose). Then add some grain or something that symbolizes money or wealth to manifest abundance in your marriage. After that, add something to symbolize health, such as a picture of someone exercising. Then add something to symbolize longevity in your marriage, such as a picture of an elderly couple holding hands. Finally, add a few drops of your favorite wine or beverage to symbolize joy and happiness.

Before you wrap up and tie the offering, blow on it three times while holding a mental image of your marriage to connect it to you energetically and to your intention. It is okay to wait a bit to burn or bury it, but don't wait more than a day or two or it will lose much of its power.

If you are guided to burn it, it is critical to do so in a safe place, such as a wood-burning fireplace (not a gas-burning one, for obvious reasons). You must also watch it until it burns completely while holding your intention for your perfect marriage in your mind. There should be no flame left, only coals, before putting the fire completely out with water so all the coals are cool to the touch. You can burn it during your fire ceremony, after the three twigs have completely burned.

If you are burying it, find a private place out of the way where it won't be disturbed and can decay fully. You can also take it to certain places, such as a mountain or near a large body of water, to boost its power if you feel a special connection to those places. The key is that you must feel a special connection to the place and be guided to bury it there.

The beauty of offerings is that you can use them as often as you like, even daily, and you can use them to manifest anything you want, from a promotion to starting a business to writing a book. As you continue to do offerings, you may notice that you are getting better at making them because they will feel more powerful and will manifest more fully and rapidly.

Sand-painting

Sand-painting is the most intuitive of the three techniques I will teach you where you will create a collection of objects on the ground that symbolically represent you and your energetic system. Done properly, a sand painting will enable you to modify the energy flows and patterns both in your system and around you by moving the objects in and out of the painting.

That said, doing a sand painting properly takes more practice, so I recommend spending time working with the fire ceremony and doing offerings first if you are new to manifesting and intuitive work.

When you feel ready to begin a sand painting, start by doing three cycles of the fire-breathing meditation and then asking Spirit where to do the painting and if you need to include any special or specific objects. You may also get instructions as to when and where to do the painting, such as at the full moon or near a mountain or body of water. The location should be in a private spot where your painting won't be disturbed, but close enough that you can return to it a couple of times over the next few days.

When you arrive at your location, clear a small area a few feet across on the bare ground. Don't place your painting on a rock or grass unless you are specifically instructed to do so. Collect objects such as sticks, small stones, and leaves from the area around your painting and use them to create a border to the painting within the bare area, leaving some room outside the border.

Spend a few minutes meditating about which objects to place in your painting. The goal is for the painting to symbolically represent you and your energy system, so the objects may not form a recognizable pattern. Keep moving objects within the painting, as well as in and out of the painting, as you feel led until you feel a sense of completion. There are no right or wrong locations for the objects; just follow your feelings until you no longer feel the urge to move anything.

Remember, you are creating a symbolic representation of yourself, not a literal picture, so it may not look like anything specific.

Next, gently blow three deep breaths on your painting while holding a mental image of yourself in your mind to connect yourself energetically to the painting. While you can continue to work on your painting after the breaths, it is often better to let the painting sit for a few hours or even overnight to allow it fully connect to your energetic system.

When you return to your sand painting, sit and meditate on your intention to marry. As you meditate, you may feel a subtle urge to move objects within the painting and to add or remove objects. Follow your subtle urges because as you shift the items in the sand painting, you are shifting both your energetic system and the energy patterns and flows around you.

Once you have a sense of completion and stop feeling the urge to move anything, leave the sand painting again for a few hours or even overnight; whichever feels right. Don't be surprised if objects in your painting seem to have moved while you were away — that is a sign that energy patterns are shifting.

It is also okay if the entire painting is washed away or simply gone. As long as you built it when and where you were led to, whatever happens is part of the manifesting process.

When you return to your sand painting the third time, sit in meditation and listen for guidance on how to dismantle the painting by removing the objects in the order you feel led to and to possibly return the objects to specific locations. It is important to follow these subtle urges because you need to disconnect the sand painting from your energetic system properly or you could be affected unintentionally and your intention may not manifest.

Sand paintings typically work quickly — in just a few days, in some cases — and can be repeated every few days if you feel urged to do so.

If Nothing Works

While all of the techniques we have discussed are powerful, there can be times when none of the techniques seems to work. If you have re-read how to perform each technique and performed each one correctly at least a few times, you may have a problem with your energy system. Your energetic system may be infected by a negative energy pattern, much like a software virus infects a computer. While it is possible to remove it yourself (sand paintings can be used to do this for example), it is usually much faster and easier to have a trained healer do it for you.

A wide variety of energy healers are capable of removing these negative energy patterns and do so on a regular basis. Shamans and Reiki masters are examples of energy healers capable of such work. The two keys to look for in a healer are formal training in their system of practice and high ethics. Specifically, their ethics should only allow them to heal people and prohibit them from doing any type of dark energy work, such as cursing or harming people.

For example, you don't want a faith healer who just discovered his gift one day out of the blue, because he probably lacks the training and techniques required for removing a specific energy pattern.

If you can't find a trained healer in your area with a good reputation and high ethics, you can always contact the Four Winds Society (thefourwinds.com) for a recommendation. Many advanced healers don't have to be physically present to heal clients and can work long distance over Skype or the phone. Such advanced healers are usually full-time practitioners and often maintain websites where you can contact them to schedule a healing session. Rates are typically $50 to $150 per hour and sessions take one to two hours for a total cost of $100-$300. Removing a negative energy pattern typically takes a single session.

Be wary of anyone who charges more than this or insists that you need extra sessions to remove a single negative energy pattern (although you can have more than one pattern). Always listen to Spirit about when you need a session and about whom you should allow to work on you. Energetic healing is also not a replacement for medical or psychiatric care, but it can complement conventional medical and psychiatry care by shifting the energetic pattern of your illness so it can be treated more easily.

Final Steps to Manifesting

Always remember that manifesting is not magic. You still have to take the basic steps, such as joining an online dating website, going on first dates with a variety of guys, and going to parties to expand your social network and meet more people. Remember that you are manifesting the perfect person for your soul, not Brad Cooper's twin. Your perfect-for-you man will pass all the other testing criteria we talked about earlier in this book, but he may not have all the extras you want, such as perfect hair, abs of steel, and a fat wallet.

Give Spirit the benefit of the doubt when he shows up, because it can take some time to see just how perfect he is for you.

In Review

- Read and apply the two previous chapters before attempting these techniques for manifesting.
- The fire ceremony is the simplest manifesting technique and is most effective when done on the night of the full moon.
- Use the "toothpick and candle" version of the fire ceremony if you don't have access to an appropriate place for a fire ceremony.
- Offerings are another relatively simple technique and can be buried or burned (as part of your fire ceremony).
- Sand-painting is the most intuitive of the three techniques discussed and should only be attempted after working with fire ceremonies and offerings.
- If these techniques aren't working (or Spirit directs you), you may have a negative energy pattern and require the assistance of a trained healer to remove it.

CHAPTER FOURTEEN

How to Know He's the One

*O*f course, Spirit is not going to go to all the trouble of bringing you the man you are meant for without providing a way for you to know that he is the one. However, you first need to make sure he meets all the requirements we've previously discussed. He must be able to delay gratification as evidenced by his good credit score, being healthy and fit, and having a commitment to his career and education. He must also be emotionally stable, as evidenced by having a secure attachment (or insecure if you are securely attached), not a disorganized attachment. Finally, he must have the correct relational archetype for you (Athlete, Engineer, Film Director, or Artist) and not be a shadow archetype (Godfather, Gamer, Rock Star, or MAW).

Only if he meets all of these requirements and you have enough chemistry that you want to marry him should you test him energetically. The reason this is the last step and comes after all of the scientific requirements is because it is actually very risky to depend on Spirit to do all the work. In fact, trying to completely depend on Spirit to do everything for you can result in Spirit deciding to teach you a lesson about common sense and doing your part.

It is better to view the scientific steps as the gifts Spirit provides to everyone, like sunshine and rain. That means Spirit expects us to make good use of these general gifts before asking for specific gifts for ourselves. While there may have been a few moments in history where Spirit provided manna from heaven, the rest of the time, Spirit expected everyone to plant crops and was willing to allow those who refused to starve.

Engaging Spirit

If everything we have previously discussed lines up and you have enough chemistry (but not crazy chemistry), here's how to test him energetically to make sure he is the one meant for you. First, ask Spirit if he is the one. If you have done all the previous exercises and developed the ability to communicate with Spirit, trust Spirit to clearly communicate the answer to you. However, if you want to be extra sure, here are two simple, yet powerful, techniques to be certain.

Pendulum Testing

Pendulum testing is perhaps the easiest way to test something energetically. It takes less than a minute and you can carry your pendulum in your pocket or purse to use whenever you have a question. (I used mine to pick out my mattress and pillow, and I sleep great now.) The only downside is that it can take up to a month to connect your pendulum to your energetic system properly so it will give you accurate answers. If you don't have that long, skip to the next section on muscle testing.

Unless you already own a pendulum, you will have to buy or make one. Pendulums can be made from almost anything. I have seen everything from a stone picked up from the ground and put on a string to a beautiful piece of jewelry. The key is that you feel a special connection to it and you are called (or instructed by Spirit) to use it. Never use someone else's pendulum — it has to be connected to your energetic system for it to provide accurate answers.

Once you have found your pendulum, you must connect it to your energetic system. Blowing on it three times every day is the simplest way, but you can deepen your connection by wearing or carrying it. You can also sleep with it under your pillow as well. Within a month, it will be deeply connected to your energetic system.

After the pendulum is connected, you have to calibrate it. Holding the pendulum in your non-dominant hand, ask a series of simple, yes/no questions that you already know the answer to. Your series of questions should have a good mix of yes and no answers so you can see what the pendulum does depending on the answer. Be sure to still the pendulum between each question so its answer is clear.

Pendulums typically swing in two of three possible ways — in a straight line to and from you, a straight line across you from left to right, or in a circle.

After you ask a question, continue holding the question in your mind for several seconds and see what the pendulum does: straight line to and from you, straight line left and right, or make a circle. You should consistently see the same action from the pendulum when the answer is yes and the opposite action when the answer is no. That way, you will know what "yes" is and what "no" is for your pendulum (mine swings in a circle for yes and left to right for no).

If you don't achieve 100% consistency, you might not be holding the question long enough (the pendulum responds to whatever thought is in your mind, not just questions), but the more likely answer is that it is not sufficiently connected to your energetic system. You can try to give it another month on your person and under your pillow, but there is no guarantee that will work, so starting over with another pendulum is a reasonable choice, too.

Once you are consistently hitting 100% accuracy for questions you know the answer to, you are ready to use your pendulum to see if a man is the one meant for you. However, you won't actually test a man until the very end of the second phase of your relationship, which we'll go over in the next chapter. When you do test a man, only ask your pendulum once a day, preferably in the morning, right after fire-breathing. If he is the one, you should get the same yes answer every day for at least a week.

If you get a consistent no every time from your pendulum, I would encourage you to trust Spirit and move on. He may be a great guy and you may be wildly attracted to him, but that doesn't make him the one meant for you. I can tell you from personal experience that someone may seem great now, but if you look back years later, you'll see how you wouldn't have been great together. However, if you just can't accept that he's not the one, you can use muscle testing, which we cover below, to double-check your answer.

If you get any variation in the answer, you need to explore that with Spirit. He may be the one, but something may have to happen before Spirit will give you the green light to move forward. Follow the message Spirit sends you, whether it is for you to do something or to wait for him to do something. In the meantime, don't keep testing him with your pendulum. Instead, wait for the issue to resolve and then repeat the week of testing to get a clear answer.

Of course, if you get variability again, you can ask Spirit and repeat the resolution process or switch to muscle testing, which we will discuss next, to see if you can get a clear answer.

Muscle-testing

Muscle-testing is bit more complicated to use than a pendulum because you need a partner to help you (such as your wingman/book buddy), but it's faster because you don't have to spend a month waiting for your pendulum to connect to your energetic system. However, you do need to wait until the end of the second phase of your relationship to test him, which we will discuss in the next chapter.

The easiest way to do muscle-testing is for you to stand with feet a shoulder's width apart and to clasp your hands while you hold them as straight as you can out in front of you. Your partner will press down on your hands while you ask a yes/no question in your mind. If the answer is yes, then your arms will stay strong and will barely move. If the answer is no, then you won't be able to resist no matter how much you try.

The strength difference between yes and no is so dramatic that when I'm demonstrating this for a group of my students, I pick the biggest and strongest person in the class and then use the tiniest girl to press down on their arms. I have seen massive bodybuilders almost be knocked over by tiny women when the answer is no, while the same bodybuilder could barely budge the arms of the smallest woman when the answer is yes.

Similarly to calibrating the pendulum, you should run through a series of yes/no questions where you know the answer to validate that you are using the technique correctly. The one caveat is to avoid questions that are associated with a negative experience, because the negative energy of the association might make you weak even if the answer is yes. For example, if you were abused as a child and one of the questions was "Did you live at xxx address as a child," the negative association with the abuse will probably make you go weak even if the answer was yes.

Once you and your partner are able to get consistently accurate answers, you can test whether your man is the One (if you are at the end of the second phase of your relationship, which we cover in the next chapter). Close your eyes and imagine being married to him. Then have your buddy push down on your hands. It should be quite clear if you are strong or weak, indicating that he is or is not the one you are meant for. You should repeat the testing a few more times to make sure you keep getting the same answer. You can also repeat the muscle-testing with a different partner and in a different location, just to be absolutely sure, but if you consistently get the same answer, you should trust it.

If you keep getting inconsistent answers, you probably need a different partner. Just pick someone who doesn't have a strong opinion about your man, so it won't affect them testing you.

If the muscle-testing keeps saying no, but you just can't accept that answer, you can ask Spirit to give you a clear message to help you accept the answer. Be open to what Spirit says and practice radical acceptance to hear the answer clearly. Just be aware that Spirit may not be saying no because he is a poor choice for marriage. In fact, he may be an amazing man to marry, but you may also have negative karma to work out together, such as a major illness or early death that Spirit is trying to protect you from. Obviously, there is no way to be sure, but you've trusted Spirit so far, so why stop now.

In Review

- Spirit expects you to use all of the scientific criteria we have previously discussed to determine whether a man is appropriate for you.
- Trust Spirit to tell you if he is the one meant for you.
- Use your pendulum to test if a man is the one meant for you (but not until the end of the second phase of your relationship).
- You can use a partner to do muscle-testing to know whether he is the one meant for you (at the end of the second phase).

STEP V

Sealing the Deal

CHAPTER FIFTEEN

Getting Him to the Altar

$\mathcal{N}$ ow that you think you have met the one, remember that he may not realize he's the one meant for you (yet). I would strongly urge you to not tell him you think he's the one, because men are skittish when it comes to marriage. If you seem too focused on marriage, he may bolt, no matter how perfect your relationship actually is.

Rather, men often have to be seduced into marriage, even though all the research shows that they are happier and healthier once they are married. That is because men do not grow up dreaming about weddings. When they imagine getting married, it typically evokes thoughts of being trapped and of all the women they will never have.

There are only three reasons why men get excited about being married:

1. They have some crazy plan for their life that includes getting married at a certain point and are excited about checking that box off.
2. They think you are so far out of their league that they want to lock you down before you wake up and dump them.
3. They don't believe in sex outside marriage and are still virgins.

Generally, most men marry because they can't live without you and know you will leave if they don't step up and marry you.

I'm not saying this to depress or scare you, just to let you know what you are up against: a stubborn mule dying of thirst that has be dragged to water. Of course, there are exceptions, but this describes the majority. Don't worry, though, because in this chapter, I show you how to hack a man's brain so the odds of getting him to the altar are solidly in your favor.

Laying the Foundation

There are four phases in getting him to the altar (with a fifth phase for the really stubborn ones), but first, let's lay some groundwork — a foundation for applying the steps. As I previously said, you can't seem too eager to get married, which is why you should always say, "If I meet the right person" when you are asked if you want to get married.

In fact, this is bigger than not appearing too eager: You should say it to everyone — friends, family, anyone who asks — and not just men you date. It should be your mantra that you tell yourself all the time, so it sinks down into the core of your soul. After all, you don't want settle, do you?

The point is that you want to convey that a man has to earn the right to marry you, not just be willing to marry you. You must know down in your core that being married to you is a privilege that must be earned on a daily basis and can never be taken for granted. You have to set high standards for any man you are with, because men have a bad habit of only living up to lowest level you will tolerate. That is why you need to always maintain your ability and willingness to walk away if his behavior ever slips.

In addition to setting a high standard for him, you also want to limit how much interest you show in him throughout most of the time before you get married. I'm not talking playing hard to get, but rather matching his interest level with slight modifications, based on his archetype. If he is a leader (i.e., Athlete or a Film Director), let him lead the relationship by showing a little bit more interest than you do as you go along. However, if you are the leader and he's the supporter, (i.e., Engineer or Artist), you need to lead your relationship by showing slightly more interest, where you take a step forward and then wait to see if he takes a step to catch up to you before you take another step.

Again, this isn't playing hard to get. It's more about showing a reasonable amount of interest given the seriousness of getting married and how little you know him, especially early on. Emotionally healthy people ease into serious relationships slowly, so being too excited and trying to move too fast only ends up scaring the good ones away. Your cool approach to dating him also subtly lets him know that you are not a candidate for something casual or for being a side chick.

> Safety note: Always remember to take appropriate safety precautions before you know someone well, such as meeting in public places and providing your own transportation to and from your dates.

Phase One: Non-exclusive Dating (0 to 3 months)

The first phase of getting him to the altar begins when you meet a man who seems like he might be the one and ends when you agree to be in an exclusive relationship together. This is the initial phase where you are going on dates together but also on dates with other people. While this phase may last up to three months after you first meet him, it could also be a matter of weeks. The deciding factor is becoming exclusive as a couple.

The primary purpose of this phase is to evaluate him to make sure he meets all the scientific requirements. Remember, you want to:

a) Make sure he's actually the appropriate archetype and not its shadow.

b) Start collecting information to see if he "ate the marshmallow." While you shouldn't share credit scores just yet (asking this too soon would be more likely to scare good men off), you can certainly determine whether he exercises and takes care of his health, and where he stands in terms of his career and education.

c) Start getting a sense of his attitude about marriage and what his purpose(s) for marriage might be. (Many online dating sites allow you to screen out people based on various criteria, including attitudes about marriage, which can help you skip the "Marriage is just a piece of paper" dance.)

After you've been on a couple of dates and if you feel a solid attraction to him (but not crazy attraction), re-read the chapter on your complementary archetype (Athlete, Engineer, Film Director, or Artist) so you have a clear sense of the qualities and traits your archetype should possess. Read the three other chapters as well to get a sense of the other archetypes to help you distinguish between them.

It should be quite obvious which archetype he is, but if you aren't totally sure, ask the buddy who's working through the book with you. If you still aren't sure or you and your buddy disagree, ask Spirit for guidance. However, Spirit may jump to the final question of whether or not he's the one meant for you instead of telling you his archetype.

Also, as you re-read the chapter on your archetype, pay careful attention to the section on his shadow. Shadows will look and feel the same to you as your archetype and will only differ in the ways described. This initial phase before you become exclusive (and absolutely before you have sex) is the best time to identify and reject a shadow because the longer you wait to get rid of him, the more time he has to work his way past your defenses and enthrall your heart with his dark magic. (If you need help breaking up with a shadow or anyone else, read the article on my website about saying no with class.)

Your next task as you date (non-exclusively) is to gather information about whether or not he "ate the marshmallow," meaning whether he shows the ability to delay gratification. You should be looking for signs that he takes care of his health by exercising and eating right while avoiding dangerous things like smoking or drinking too much (or any drug use at all). You should also ask him about his education and career to see if he has applied himself by putting in the time to become good at something that he can make a living at, whether it's programming computers or plumbing.

Also, look for signs of how he manages his money. Does he drive an expensive vehicle (if he's under 50 and isn't a trust fund kid, he should be stacking his paper instead of spending it on his ride) or does he drive a rust-bucket because his credit is so bad (or he's that committed to saving his money)? Similarly, did he over-pay for a fancy apartment or condo, or did he invest in a house in a rising area (or is fixing one up to flip)? You can also ask him about the story behind any bling he's wearing to see if it was a gift or if he dropped serious dough on it. The key to watch for is whether he is good with his money or tends to spend it all.

The last goal of this initial phase is to get a sense of his dreams and plans for his life, especially in terms of marriage. Just like you, he should be open to marriage if he meets the right person. You just need to watch out for extreme answers, such as he's never getting married (or getting married again) because "marriage is for chumps" or that marriage is "just a piece of paper." These aren't absolute deal-breakers, but it does mean you will have to be tougher with him and might have to walk away if he doesn't eventually come around.

Don't worry, though: A lot of this anti-marriage talk is just manly bluster, and this chapter was designed to crack tough nuts. You just have to stick to the plan.

You can also learn about what his purpose(s) for a marriage might be – raising a family, building a career, travel, etc. – by asking about his dreams for his life. You can also ask him questions like, "What would you do if you won the lottery?" or "If all your dreams came true, what would your life look like in five years and in 10 years?" Alternatively, you can ask what he would wish for if he had three wishes. These questions take away the barriers and his doubts so you can see the deepest dreams for his life.

Do your best not to react positively or negatively to what he says, because you don't want him to edit or restrict what he says in any way. Also, he may not want to reveal how he really feels just yet, so watch for signs that what he's talking about actually excites him. A lack of genuine excitement, combined with him saying something that excites you, should send up the red flag that he is just telling you what you want to hear.

Listen for what he is passionate about when he is talking at other times. Does he keep talking about his travels and where he wants to go next? Does he keep taking about climbing the ladder at work or wanting to be wealthy? These are clues to what he really cares about, which may not be the same as what he said his dreams are about.

Don't worry just yet if his purposes for marriage don't seem to line up with yours. It is not unusual for a person to develop a strong interest in something after being exposed to it through a partner. Just start to share your purposes for marriage in the form of your dreams for your life to give your purposes some time to gel and merge naturally.

We'll discuss how to negotiate and merge your purposes as your relationship progresses if that becomes necessary in Phase IV, later in this chapter.

Again, the length of this phase can be highly variable, but it shouldn't be longer than three months or shorter than three weeks (with a minimum of three dates). If he is a leader (i.e., Athlete or Film Director), you should keep all of your dating options open during this phase and continue to meet and date other men until he asks for an exclusive relationship.

However, if you are the leader and he's the supporter (i.e., Engineer or Artist), you will need to move things along. Once you are sure he is the right archetype for you and not a shadow, and it doesn't look like he ate the marshmallow, you can start moving toward an exclusive relationship. If you are a masculine leader and he's an Artist, you can just tell him you want to be in an exclusive relationship.

However, if you are a feminine leader and he's an Engineer, you will need to give him permission to ask for an exclusive relationship by dropping hints. If he is a strong supporter with no leadership tendencies, tell him he needs to ask you for an exclusive relationship. Just don't be surprised if he looks at you funny because he thought you already were exclusive.

(It is a common relationship issue with Engineers, and to some degree with Artists, that they think so much about things that they forget to verbalize their thoughts and share them with you. That's a bad habit that has to be unlearned. Just start training them now to "use your words.")

Before we go any further, let's take a moment to talk about sex. If you are a feminine leader, feminine supporter, or masculine supporter (i.e., dating an Engineer, Athlete, or Film Director), you will want to delay having sex throughout this period. Save it for after you are in an exclusive relationship. This is not out of some antiquated since of morality. You can have all the side hookups you want with guys you know are not the one (just don't let the sex change your mind). You just need to wait with your potential husband because you don't want to risk turning into a side chick or for the sex to cloud your good judgment as you assess him. So many women have been manipulated into overlooking major character flaws and red flags in a man because of how good he is in bed. The world doesn't need another sequel.

If you are a masculine leader pursuing your Artist, your playbook is a bit different. You don't need to wait for sex with him unless you know you tend to fall for guys after getting intimate. I just recommend waiting long enough to gather the appropriate information regarding his ability to delay gratification (eating the marshmallow) and to ensure he is an Artist and not a MAW (a shadow) because MAWs can be hard to get rid of once you've bonded sexually.

This all sounds nice and neat, but what if he shows all the signs of being the one (pending his credit score and separation test) and then won't ask you for an exclusive relationship after dating for three months (or agree to one if he is an Artist)?

First, know down deep in your soul that three months is plenty of time for a man to figure out if he wants an exclusive relationship with you. Second, recognize that there is only one way to change a man's mind about being in committed relationship, and that is to give him a solid dose of life without you in it.

Sit him down and let him know that you are looking for a serious relationship and are not interested in dating for the sake of dating.

If he still won't agree to an exclusive relationship, refuse to meet him the next time he calls to ask you out. Remind him that you are looking for a serious relationship and are not interested in dating for the sake of dating. Give him one more month to ask for an exclusive relationship (while you keep going on dates with other guys). If he still hasn't come around after a month, block his number because he's not offering anything you want.

Phase II: Exclusive Dating (3 to 6 Months)

This is the phase where your relationship really gets going. During the early part of this phase, you need to focus on filling any gaps left in your evaluation of him. You should be checking out his health and fitness habits (don't be fooled by how he looks, because youth and good genes can cover up all manner of bad habits), and his career prospects.

You should also be starting to talk about how you both manage your money and getting a sense of whether he is a saver or a spender. You can also bring up credit scores now, not to grill him, but rather to see how he reacts. Does he even know what his credit score is? If not, you can encourage him to find out (which may lead to him sharing without you asking).

The key to these early money discussions is that they are low-pressure and involve gradually exchanging more and more information about both of your finances from how much you make to your monthly expenses to how much debt you both have.

However, if he just won't share anything at all about his finances, be patient and give him some time to see if he starts sharing once he knows you better. Some people are raised to believe that talking about money is rude (or private). Just know that you can't get married until you have a detailed discussion about his finances, including sharing his current credit score.

You also want to continue to explore his future plans for his life in regard to marriage, and where he sees his career going. If he is still adamantly opposed to marriage and isn't showing any signs of softening, you have an important decision to make: whether to play along and try to soften him later or to try to change his mind now.

If he seems to be softening by being less intense in his opposition or he starts to say "Maybe," then you are better off waiting to see if he will continue to open up to the possibility of marriage as he gets to know you. You should still be open about your intention to be married because it will help him decide if he wants to be with you. Most men will break up with you if they just can't see themselves getting married, and the ones who won't tend to be shadows or have attachment issues that will become clear over time (and you should break up with them for that reason).

If he is not softening, but you feel confident in your ability to walk away later, check in with Spirit by testing him, using your pendulum or by doing muscle-testing. If you get a consistently positive answer, you can proceed, but if you get a consistently negative answer, trust Spirit and let him go.

The tougher case is if you get variable answers, which can mean he is on the fence and can go either way. In that case, it is up to you, but be prepared to walk away at any moment. You should also keep testing him on a monthly basis to see which way he is leaning and to know whether it is safe to continue or if you need to let him go.

If he is not softening and you don't feel confident in your ability to walk away later because you attach to people quickly, you should take the risk of trying to change his mind now. Sit him down and be clear that your ultimate goal is marriage. Let him know that he doesn't have to decide now if you are the one, but he must be willing to get married at some point if he wants to keep seeing you. Let him know that he has a month to decide if he's willing to eventually get married.

If he doesn't break up with you immediately, keep seeing him, but stick to walking away after a month if he doesn't come around. After you walk away, you can keep taking his phone calls for another month to see if he's changed his mind, but don't see him or talk very long on the phone with him because it will just give him more opportunity to sway you. If he still hasn't come around after a month of talking on the phone, stop taking his phone calls and get back to dating and meeting other people.

At some point during this phase, the question of children will probably come up. You don't have to agree right now; you just don't want to be at opposite ends of the spectrum from each other. In other words, if you think you'd like kids, it's okay if he's ambivalent, but it's not good if he's certain he doesn't want kids. However, a lot of people (maybe even you) have trouble thinking about children before they are with the right person. It's okay to wait to sort this out as long as you are not diametrically opposed.

Similarly, you want to see if your plans for your lives are compatible and if you can find a common purpose or two that will support your marriage, as we discussed in Chapter 2. Again, things don't have to line up perfectly at this point, but they shouldn't be at opposite ends or completely incompatible with each other. For example, he shouldn't want to buy a sailboat to sail around the world while you want to start an organic farm.

Try hard to keep this a gradual exchange of information without judgment. You never know, because he may come to love your idea for an organic farm and be satisfied with the occasional vacation cruise on a sailboat.

If either or both of you already have children, this is the earliest you should introduce them to him or for you to meet his (although waiting is fine). Ideally, you just want to meet in passing and you don't want to spend any significant amount of time together right now for a few reasons.

First, meeting your new love is stressful for your child because children often have secret fantasies that their parents will get back together. Second, children also tend to see your new love as competition, so they often act up to keep your attention. Third, if you are with your new love, be aware of how much attention you are giving your child if you are making googly eyes at your new love. It's better to wait until it is clear you are heading toward marriage before you put your children through the stress of getting to know him (or his kids).

This is also when you will probably have sex for the first time. I'm not recommending you have sex now if it's against your beliefs or you don't feel ready. I'm just saying this is the earliest time that it is okay to have sex (unless you are a masculine leader dating an Artist, as I explained previously).

If you decide to test the waters, don't expect him to blow your mind the very first time. It's actually a bit of a red flag if he does, because generally only players have amazing sex skills and can knock it out of the park on their first swing. It is normal for it to take some time and practice to get to know each other's bodies, which is why a bad first experience is not a death knell for your relationship. Give yourself some time to see how it evolves before you make a decision about your compatibility in bed.

Once you start having sex regularly (if you aren't putting it off for some reason), it is time for the separation test. To help you determine his attachment style, plan a weekend trip (or whenever you would normally spend the entire day together) without him to see how he responds. Go back and review Chapter 4 if you are fuzzy on the details of attachment theory and how your man should respond to the separation test.

The key is to make sure you are gone when he doesn't have some big event or plan to keep him busy. When you tell him about the separation, don't suggest a plan for how you will stay in touch. Instead, see what he suggests.

Secure guys may seem a little sad because they will miss you, but they don't insist on a strict schedule of contact. Insecure guys usually try to talk you out of the separation by suggesting they tag along or even trying to convince you not to go. If they can't, they usually insist on a strict schedule of contact, such as every night before you go to bed. However, occasionally, they will play it cool, but then they'll blow up your phone or do something weird to let you know they are insecure.

Disorganized guys can do anything from turning cold and acting completely indifferent to getting upset and starting a big fight then and there. (The fight can be about anything and may not seem to be about the trip, at least not on the surface.) However, you should have spotted a disorganized guy before now from his lack of stable friendships and close relationships with family.

While you are gone on your trip, completely ignore the contact plan and don't call or text him the entire time you are gone to see what he does. Avoid contacting him if he seems fine with the separation and doesn't suggest a plan. While you are gone, don't even pick up your phone if he calls or respond to his texts (beyond a "We're fine and having fun" so he knows you are physically safe). The secure guy will be cool about you not following the schedule or responding, and will probably just shoot you a text or two that he misses you and can't wait to see you, or leave a sweet voice-mail to that effect.

The insecure guy will have more trouble with your lack of contact and responsiveness. Mr. Ambivalent/Dramatic will either get highly upset while you are gone or after you get back, while Mr. Avoidant/Reserved will seem okay while you are gone, but act like your relationship is over when you see him again until you reassure him otherwise. Mr. Ambivalent/Dramatic may also surprise you and show up wherever you went.

In addition to blowing up your phone, the Disorganized guy will react in some extreme way, from showing up wherever you went to even stalking you. Alternatively, he may accuse you of cheating while you were gone or cheat himself. He may also pick a big fight over nothing and then break up with you over it. The point is that he will react badly to the separation. Just don't be surprised if he tries to blame his weirdness on you and make you feel like you did something wrong for leaving.

Now that you have a sense of your man's attachment style (Secure, Insecure-Ambivalent, Insecure-Avoidant, or Disorganized — see Chapter 4 for a refresher), you will need to respond to that information based on your own attachment style. If he is securely attached, you are good to go. If he is Disorganized, you need to run like hell. However, if he is one of the insecure types, you'll need to look at the score you got on the attachment scale in Chapter 4 to know whether you will work well enough together.

If you are securely attached (0–5), he can be either of the insecure styles, just not Disorganized, because you will heal him over time. If you are in the gray zone between secure and insecure (6–10), he will need to be at least in the gray zone himself, if not securely attached, or he may pull you down into his drama. If you have an insecure attachment (11–20), then you have to go for a securely attached man who seems a bit dull and boring, or you can go to psychotherapy for a year or so to shift your attachment style in a secure direction.

If you have a deeply insecure or possibly disorganized style (20 and up), you should be working on finding and working with a psychotherapist and only reading this for future reference, because you are probably not ready to have a healthy relationship yet.

During this phase, your relationship should be deepening as you grow closer. You should be trying out each other's interests and spending the night together from time to time (but not every night, because you need to continue to evaluate him and not rush ahead). Just keep a careful eye out for any signs of a harem or side chicks. He may introduce them as friends, but trust your instincts. You should also be meeting his friends to see what they are like, and letting your friends meet him. Listen to what your sanest friends (securely attached and didn't eat the marshmallow) think of him and whether they think you two work as a couple.

If everything checks out (he seems good with money, takes care of his health, has good career prospects, is emotionally stable, and is the appropriate archetype and not a shadow), now is the time to test him energetically using the techniques discussed in Chapter 14. Start with asking Spirit after fire-breathing meditation. If Spirit gives permission to proceed, you can make preparations for testing him with either your pendulum or muscle-testing with a partner.

If you get consistently positive answers, keep going, but if you get inconsistent answers or a clear negative answer, follow my advice in Chapter 14 to clarify the situation. Alternatively, if you use prayer to help guide you in making important decisions, now is the time to reach out to whatever higher power you believe in.

Phase III: The Dark Side (6 to 9 months)

Phase III typically begins about six months after you first met and is characterized by the new car smell wearing off. What I mean is that someone can stay on his best behavior and hide his dark side for about six months. After that, cracks start appearing in the dam and the dark side starts leaking through. It is normal to put our best foot forward when a relationship is new, but over time we naturally let our true colors show.

This is when you will have to decide whether you can live with his annoying habit of leaving the toilet seat up and his aversion to doing laundry or dishes (or his obsession with cleaning and being organized). You'll also have to decide if you can cope with each other's food issues, such as if one of you is vegan and the other lives for steak.

This is where being with a divorced guy is actually a benefit, because he is probably already house-broken and is familiar with the issues that typically annoy women. Bachelors who've never been married or lived with a woman are often clueless and can take years to master the basics of keeping a home clean and functional.

However, while you can train him to put the toilet seat down, change on a more fundamental level is much more rare. In fact, the critical decision you have to make here is to decide whether you can cope with him exactly as he is. While it is possible he will change, it is far more likely that any change will be glacial and only happen over decades, if it ever happens at all. If you can honestly say that you could live with him exactly as he is for the rest of your life, then you are in good shape. Otherwise, you need to sit down with him now and see if he is willing and able to change before you go any further.

The other key event in this phase is your first big argument. I'm not talking about some minor disagreement, but a real argument where you both get mad and maybe even yell a bit. This is a valuable event, because it shows you how you each argue and fight, as well as how you make up. Being able to argue appropriately without any cheap shots at each other, making threats, or losing control physically is critical for every successful couple. It's also important that neither of you give in too easily, because failing to stand your ground at all and compromising immediately to avoid the argument just leads to resentment that will fester and eventually explode in a truly destructive rage.

When healthy and mature couples argue, no one attacks the other person's character or belittles the other during the argument. They also don't attack each other verbally for the purpose of causing emotional pain. They don't show contempt for the other or stonewall the other by refusing to discuss the issue. Similarly, no one threatens to end the relationship or tries to retaliate or seek revenge in any way. Finally, no one becomes violent or threatens to be violent in any way.

This is especially important for you as a woman, because any hint of violence in him is a bad sign, and even if you just feel unsafe, you must take that feeling seriously. If a man hits you or physically intimidates you, he will never stop, no matter how much he promises to change or begs for forgiveness. Hitting and intimidation are buried so deeply in a man's character that it is almost easier to break a horrible drug addiction than it is to stop hitting and intimidating. He may sincerely want to change, but it takes years of intense work to do so. That is why you should have a zero-tolerance policy and bless him with the years alone that it takes to change such a deep-seated issue.

In contrast, good men maintain control and won't intimidate you in any way. If a good man gets upset, he will merely walk away to cool down before continuing the argument without slamming his fists or breaking things. You just need to let him step back to calm down and trust that he will come back when he's ready to continue.

This is the one time you should absolutely ignore the advice to never go to bed angry. If he needs to sleep on it before you continue, give him the time. There has been many a morning where I have woken up happy to concede and compromise when I was completely unwilling to do so the night before.

It is also important to see how you make up after the fight. It is a positive sign if you both apologize for anything you said during the argument that was even mildly harsh. It is also a positive sign if both of you spontaneously affirm how much you love each other and that you absolutely want to be together. The compromise that resolves the issue should be easily negotiated at this point. There should not be any lingering resentment afterward. Don't be surprised if you feel closer after the argument is over.

You shouldn't expect to argue perfectly at this point, but you do want to make sure there are no red flags in terms of how you argue. Marriage therapy is particularly good at teaching couples how to argue well, as long as neither of you engages in any of the major problem behaviors we've already discussed. That means no one is taking cheap shots, trying to hurt the other, threatening to end the relationship, or intimidating or hitting the other.

If either of you is doing any of these things regularly when you argue, you can try couples counseling, but generally these behaviors are signs of deeper personality issues. Such issues tend to be difficult to change during a relationship and often require a significant amount of individual psychotherapy while being alone. It is often easier to start over with someone new in such situations, because there is no guarantee of success when you are trying to change someone's personality, no matter how long you work at it.

The final task of this phase is to share your credit scores if you haven't already done so. You don't want to wait any longer, because he may need time to improve his score (you should have started improving yours long before you met him). Marriage merges your finances and credit scores in ways that divorce and even death cannot unravel. You absolutely don't want to marry him until he gets his finances and credit cleaned up.

As I said in Chapter Three, don't marry him until his score is over 700. Even if his bad credit score is due to his crazy ex-wife who was terrible with money, he still has to clean it up first. You have to be clear about your standard now and let him know you will never marry anyone with bad credit. He needs to take your requirement seriously and start working hard to get his score over 700. Otherwise, walk away because he's not husband material and is only going to drag you down into the quicksand of living hand to mouth under unrelenting financial stress.

Phase IV: The Home Stretch (9 to 12 months)

If you make it through the dark side without ignoring or compromising over any red flags, you have one last hard task to do together (and one fairly easy task after he proposes). Now is the time to offer him amnesty for keeping any secrets or making any mistakes early on in your relationship. Maybe he was sleeping with someone else right up until the last minute before you became an exclusive couple. Maybe one of his female friends is a former girlfriend or booty call. Sit him down and let him know that now is his one chance to be forgiven for all those embarrassing things that he didn't want to tell you before because they would upset you.

Yes, you'll probably be upset about them, but it's better to know them now before you get married so you can deal with them and forgive him. This also means you will get to observe how he makes these issues right to see if he has the integrity necessary to be a great husband. The key here is to make sure he knows that any future revelations will result in a much more negative response and may result in divorce because he didn't tell you when he had the chance.

However, the deeper purpose of your amnesty program is to find out if he is hiding any deal-breakers (i.e., history of cheating, spending problem, health problem, love child, sexually transmitted disease, etc.). You may think this is manipulative and unfair, but if he's not hiding anything, then he has nothing to worry about. The point is that you need to know now if he has integrity or not because men rarely tell a single lie. Uncovering a single secret often leads to more secrets. After all, do you want a man you can trust with your very life or one who is merely discreet?

If you later uncover a serious secret that he did not voluntarily reveal during your amnesty program, then you have a difficult choice to make. Lying to women is such a serious problem in men that you probably need to dump him. Research studies have shown that up to 75% of men admitted that they would lie about something important to their wives or girlfriends if they knew they would never be caught. Even worse, up to 25% admitted they would still lie even if they might get caught. So many women later regret not walking away when they had the chance. Don't be like them and lie to yourself about him changing, because it only gets harder to leave the longer you stay together.

If you make it through your amnesty program, then you get to move to the happy parts of what is usually the final phase of getting him to the altar. You should be making long-term plans together and going to important functions like work parties and family gatherings together as a couple. Pay attention to how you feel as you introduce him to your colleagues or your boss. If you don't feel proud to introduce him, what are you missing?

Meeting each other's family is a major part of this phase because his family is part of the package if you marry him. Watch how he deals with your family as he gets to know them. Is he comfortable (or at least able to cope) with your family, or do they continue to overwhelm and stress him even after he gets to know them? This is not a deal-breaker; just know that you will either be spending time with your family without him or not seeing your family as much.

Another important question is whether he can stand up to his family. Eventually, you and his mother will disagree about something and he will have to take sides. She may have given birth to him, but that doesn't mean she gets to own him. Watch how he relates to her because you don't want to find out he's a hopeless mama's boy 10 years down the road.

Speaking of family, if either or both of you already have children, now is the time to let everyone get to know each other. While they've probably already met at some point, you shouldn't have let him spend much time around your children yet and vice versa. This can be a complicated subject and almost deserves its own book, but I've written a number of articles about this on my website, www.scottcarrollmd.com, to help single parents.

The main thing to do as they get to know each other is for him to just be an adult friend, allow that friendship to develop naturally, and avoid letting him take on any kind of a parental role. Few things will upset your kids more than for your new love to try to act like their dad.

Perhaps the best parts of this phase are the little signs that you are moving toward marriage. He may start making Freudian slips where he accidently introduces you as his fiancée or says things like, "When we are married ..." Don't be surprised if one or more of your rings disappears or if he keeps trying your rings on his fingers. He may also "casually" steer you into the wedding ring section of a jewelry store or pull up rings online to see what you like. Just don't be a digger and insist on a giant stone. One carat is generally big enough – and there are better things to do with your money.

This phase, of course, begins to wind down once he proposes (if he's an Athlete or a Film Director), which should happen at right about a year (but not earlier than nine months). If the winter holidays are coming, he may be planning to ask then, so don't panic if it's already been a year. Similarly, there are some other situations where he may not ask as you come up on a year, so that shouldn't worry you.

The most common issue is if he is under 25 years old. The male brain rarely matures before 25 years old, so unless you are more than 10 years older than him and your clock is screaming at you, let his brain mature before you start pressuring him to put a ring on it.

Another common reason is that he is still in school, such as graduate school or law school. Many men have an unconscious belief that they shouldn't get married until they are done with school and are ready to take care of a family financially. If he's got less than a year to go, I would suggest waiting for him to finish, assuming everything else checks out. However, it's a more complicated situation if he has over a year or even several years to go. We'll discuss how to handle this situation in the next section, on how to deal with men that won't commit.

If you are a feminine leader and he's an Engineer, you may have to give him permission to propose by dropping some strong hints that it is time. If he is a strong supporter, you may have to get explicit with him about it. Just be sure to go with him when he shops for a ring, because he may come back with some hideous ring that is made out of space-age metals with laser etching if you don't.

Of course, if you are a masculine leader, you can propose to your Artist when you feel ready. My advice is to still go through all the steps previously outlined, including the amnesty test, because you still want to marry a quality man and divorce is painful and difficult. Just make sure you drop plenty of hints about your plans well in advance. You don't want to surprise him and risk triggering his fears of being controlled or dominated, and have him run and hide from you. Be careful here, because if he runs, you may not be able to get him back and will have to start over.

Once you are engaged is the time to negotiate your purposes for marriage. The reason why you should wait so long to do this is because your interests and purposes for your life together will merge naturally over the year or more you've dated, which will make the negotiation much easier (if you even need to at all). Once the excitement of the proposal settles down, check in with him again about his dreams for his life.

If there are any significant differences in your purposes, discuss how you can compromise or accommodate your different interests. For example, if he wants to live by the beach and you want to live near family, maybe you can agree to live near family and then vacation at the beach at least once a year, or vice versa. (However, as a parent, I will say it really helps to live near family if you have a child because nannies, day care, and babysitters get expensive.)

Similarly, if you both have high-powered careers, you may want to figure out which one to focus on or decide to try to keep up with both at the same time. Just be aware that careers tend to be incredibly important to leaders (i.e., Athletes and Film Directors) because it is a major part of their identity. You may be better off focusing on his career in that case. If he's a supporter (i.e., Engineer or Artist), he'll probably be fine supporting your career.

This is also when you need to resolve any differences in your desire for children. Obviously, this can be a contentious issue. As you work through this issue, be aware that not having children when you want them causes a profound sadness for both males and females, whereas people who don't want kids tend to do better with having kids than they think they will.

When people don't want kids, it is often based on their experiences with other people's children (or complete lack of experience), but it's different when it is your kid. It was like this with my wife. She never wanted kids before we met because she had three younger siblings growing up and her mom ran a daycare in their home, but I talked her into it and now my wife loves being a mom more than she ever imagined she would. I also have many male friends and students with a similar experience — they didn't think they wanted kids, but then ended up loving being a dad.

Phase V: If You Missed the Boat (> 1 year)

If you've always been clear that your goal was to get married if you met the right person, it is okay to ask him what he is waiting for if it's been over a year (assuming he's at least 25 years old and there isn't a big holiday coming up soon — you don't want to spoil his surprise!). You may get a variety of answers, but there are two common reasons why men wait to get married.

Many men want to wait until they have finished their education and start working in their careers to get married, especially if they are still in their 20s. If he is under 30 and still in school, don't worry too much about what he says unless he insists that he's never getting married or doesn't see the point to getting that piece of paper. It is okay to wait until he graduates or turns 30, whichever comes first; just don't move in with him until he proposes, because you need to be able to maintain your ability to walk away if he doesn't follow through and because men use living together to avoid getting married all the time.

However, if he's over 25 and done with school, or over 30 and still hasn't asked you to marry him, you need to sit him down and ask him when he is going to propose. If he doesn't give you a clear timeframe (like the ring's on order or he was waiting for your upcoming trip together), let him know that you want to get married and that you are not interested in dating for dating's sake. Give him a month to think about it and then ask him again when he's going to ask you. If he still doesn't give you an acceptable answer (there are a variety of acceptable answers, but we'll cover them in a few paragraphs), you need to give him a taste of life without you — except this time, you want to give him the maximal chance to turn it around, which means you must wait for three months to see if he comes around.

I know this sounds like a long time, but if everything checks out and Spirit is telling you he's the One, then what is three months compared to the rest of your life? You need to wait this long because men can distract themselves with hobbies and work for up to two months and won't really start missing you until the third month. Don't call him, but its okay to talk to him when he calls; just remain non-committal about getting back together and reassert your desire to be married. He may do his best to talk you out of marriage, but stand firm. Trust that if he calls at all, he'll probably propose.

However, if he hasn't proposed by the end of the third month, start joining dating websites and going on dates with other guys, even if it's just for show and you are still grieving over him. If he still hasn't proposed by the end of the fourth month, you need to bless him and let him go. Check in with Spirit on the best way to cut your energetic connection to him. You may need to do a sand painting or an offering, but your emotional recovery can still take another three to four months before you feel significantly better.

However, before you give him a three-month vacation, just be aware that there is one exception to the previous strategy. There is a small minority of men who have rigid ideas about marriage and refuse to get married before a certain age, typically 30. They may have met their future wife when they were 20 and have no doubt that they will marry her, but can't bring themselves to do it before they turn 30. Nothing you can do, from endless tears to breaking up with them, will get them to change their minds.

There is only one way to deal with such stubborn mules: Tell him that you will compromise and wait until he's 30 to actually get married if and only if he commits to marriage and puts a ring on it (assuming you're willing to wait that long). Doing this involves significant risk, so you have to be confident he will follow through and marry you. You also need an insurance policy in the form of being close to his family. (It also doesn't hurt if his family lets him know that they love you so much they are keeping you, no matter what.)

While you are engaged and waiting to get married, you should live together so you can entwine your lives so thoroughly both financially and socially that breaking up would be as complicated as getting a divorce. Just don't have a child with him until you are legally married (if that is part of your future plans together). Way too many men see having a baby mama as an acceptable life style choice, so don't expect to get married just because you get pregnant. There's also the fact that raising a child really takes two people. Trust me, you don't want to try to do it by yourself if you don't have to.

If your man just won't ask you to marry him and keeps saying it's just a piece of paper, he may have a terminal case of marriage phobia. Such a guy often has been so severely traumatized by either his own or his parents' divorce that he has panic attacks when he thinks about marriage.

Many people will tell you that you don't have to be married, that being committed to each other is enough, but I disagree.

One of my students was in this situation with her previous relationship. She was in a long-term committed relationship with a guy for over 10 years. They did everything together, traveled together, remodeled her house together, but he absolutely refused to get married. About the only thing they argued about was his refusal to say "for better or for worse." Ultimately, he knew himself better than she did, because after she got sick and had major surgery, he literally took one look at the blood gushing from her incision and disappeared. He left her at home alone while she was bleeding heavily and wouldn't even call the ambulance. She had to drag herself across the floor to get her phone and call 911 herself.

If a guy refuses to get married, there may be a very good reason. Just accept that he is making the right choice for himself and wish him well. Check in with Spirit on how to best disconnect his energy field from yours and give yourself the time to grieve. It is quite normal to be extremely sad and depressed for up to three months, but after that, you should gradually start feeling better and be back to your old self by six months.

If it is taking longer, then you should see a psychotherapist or counselor to help you complete your grieving process (see Appendix 2 to help you find one). Just trust that it is never too late to marry the man you are meant for because Spirit can fully manifest him for you when the time is right.

In Review

- Men are stubborn and skittish about marriage, so "if you meet the right one" should be your mantra.
- Phase 1 starts when you meet, lasts up to three months, and consists of non-exclusive dating where you keep seeing other people.
- Phase II starts by the three-month point and lasts about three months where you date exclusively, and do the separation test to determine his attachment style.
- Phase III starts after you've been together at least six months where the new car smell wears off and you see if you can argue well.
- Phase IV starts when you've been together at least nine months and culminates in him proposing, but only if he passes the amnesty test.
- Phase V covers how to deal with particularly stubborn men if you've been together over a year, but still aren't engaged.

CHAPTER SIXTEEN

Advice for a Successful Marriage

*I*n this last chapter, I'd like to share the most helpful advice I know for newly married couples. These are the little things I've learned over the years that help a marriage go much more smoothly and prevent a lot of problems before they start. While this is not an exhaustive list, it will still take you a long way toward a successful marriage.

1) **You can be right or be in love.** Being right is big for men, so they really need to learn this, but women can be attached to being right as well. The point is that you can focus on being right and winning arguments, or you can be understanding and have a happy marriage, but not both. In fact, it's a good idea to apologize twice as much for being right as for being wrong, because criticism that is on target hurts far more than criticism that isn't.

2) **Be gentle with each other.** When you love someone, you take them into your heart, inside your emotional defenses. When he loves you, everything you do and say touches his heart unimpeded, so touch gently. A strong word or negative comment hurts far more coming from you than from anyone else, including friends and family.

If you have something hard, but important, to say, wait until you are calm and no longer upset to say it, so you can be gentle. I'm not saying that you should be a doormat and let him wipe his feet on you; just to speak gently from a loving space. Pick the kindest words you can and wait for a time when he is best able to hear you to say what you need to say. Encourage him to follow your example.

3) **Live within your means and always save.** Money is the source of so much conflict in marriage that it deserves its own book, but the critical point is that it is good be frugal and to save as much as you can. This shouldn't be too hard if you both have good credit scores, but the best tip I can give is to resist the temptation to increase your spending just because you get a raise or you come into some extra money. The best thing to do is to maintain your current lifestyle and spending, and use the extra money for savings and investments.

Financial issues are critically important and tend to get more complicated as you get older and as you save for retirement. There is a lot to know when it comes to money and it can take years of study to become knowledgeable. Don't wait until you have a lot of money to learn about money. If you wait until then, it's too late. Your financial structures and knowledge have to be in place before you have the money they are built for, so start learning now, even if you don't have much at the moment.

4) **Never spend money to make each other happy.** Other than spending money on marriage counseling if you hit a rough patch, don't spend money to cover up problems in your relationship. It is very tempting to spring for flowers or a fancy dinner to make up for a mistake or smooth over an argument, because that works like a charm. The problem is that the good feelings you are buying are temporary. As soon as they wear off, you have to spend more money to bring them up again.

Eventually, you will get into serious debt if you do that to fix every problem or disagreement that comes up or if you try to boost chronic unhappiness in your marriage by spending money. Instead, learn to work through your problems the hard way by talking things out and having the courage to admit your faults. Learn how to enjoy being with each other so even the simplest things you do together make you happy and strengthen your bond.

5) **Have sex and orgasms as frequently as you can.** Sex (especially when you orgasm) triggers the release of many chemicals in the brain that cause you to bond to your man. Sex does similar things to him as well. However, that bonding slowly fades the longer you go without sex. Regular sex helps keep your bond strong. In fact, the six weeks you have to wait after giving birth should ideally be the longest you ever abstain, but even then, you should be creative and give each other orgasms frequently.

Obviously, there are situations where refraining from sex is necessary, such as serious illness and injury or because of infidelity or a serious conflict. Makeup sex after an argument is fine, but only after the argument is over and you've forgiven each other. Ignoring your feelings and having sex when you are still angry and don't want to be touched is risky because it can create a negative association and an aversion to having sex with him.

If the anger and lack of desire for sex persists for more than a few weeks, you need to start looking for a marriage counselor right away, because it only takes a few months of abstinence to do serious damage to your relationship. If it involves infidelity, you will almost certainly need the assistance of a marriage counselor, but we'll talk about infidelity later in this chapter.

6) **Always be willing to go to therapy.** If the two of you have a problem that is persistent and you are not able to make good progress solving it on your own, go to therapy. Therapy can work wonders, but it takes time to work. Waiting only makes it harder to solve the problem. If you wait until you are on your way to divorce court, you are far too late.

I have a simple rule for marriage: Both people must be willing to go to couples counseling or individual psychotherapy if the other person asks them, whether they think they need it or not. If one person refuses to go when their partner asks them, it makes me seriously doubt their commitment to the marriage. Personally, I would never marry someone who was unwilling to go to therapy if I asked them to.

Infidelity

My final thoughts that I want to share involve the tough subject of infidelity. Infidelity is probably the most serious challenge a marriage can face. It is often a mortal wound for a marriage and, at a minimum, it is extremely difficult for a marriage to recover from such a damaging event, no matter how much both of you may want the marriage to survive. There is no guarantee that you will be able to forgive or let it go, no matter how hard he works to earn your trust back.

I will never forget the elderly woman I met in the ER who was dragged in by the police because she attacked her husband in a grocery store. He'd had an affair over 30 years earlier. She absolutely loved him and had long since forgiven him, but her heart couldn't forget, no matter what she did. She was embarrassed and remorseful in the ER, but little things he did or said would set her off despite years of therapy.

My point is some wounds can't always be healed. When it comes to infidelity, an ounce of prevention is worth a pound of cure or, in this case, 10,000 pounds of cure. Since prevention is the key. Here are some steps to help you.

First, accept that no one has perfect willpower. If there is a bag of your favorite cookies in your kitchen, you may be able to resist 99% of the time, but eventually, you will wake up in the middle the night with the munchies and say "What the hell."

Similarly, if you keep putting yourself in situations where you have the opportunity to have an affair, it will eventually happen, no matter how strong your willpower is. The trick is to not put yourself in situations where something can happen. No private workout sessions with your amazingly fit personal trainer. No after-hour massages by the hottest massage therapist in town.

However, avoiding compromising situations is harder than you might think. The workplace is ground zero for affairs. Research suggests that up to 85% of all affairs start in the workplace, so you have to be especially careful at work.

That means never working late at the office with anyone of the opposite gender. If you have to work on a project with someone, make sure the two of you are in a public place like a coffee shop where other people can see you. If you go out of town for a meeting or conference, avoid being alone with anyone. Don't go to dinner with anyone unless you can go as a group. Don't drink alcohol (or do any drugs) when traveling alone because they make people stupid and horny.

You even have to be careful with platonic relationships. You may think of your guy friend as a brother, but if we are totally honest with ourselves, there is almost always at least a tiny amount of attraction. All it takes is a fight with your spouse, your understanding friend, and a little alcohol to grease the wheels. Next thing you know you're waking up naked in each other's arms wondering how the hell did that just happen.

You also have to be careful with platonic relationships for another reason: because emotional affairs can be almost as damaging as sexual ones. No male friend (or family member) should know the intimate details of your marriage, especially if you are having problems. Save it for your therapist. Therapists are trained to be objective and they follow strict rules about not interacting with clients outside of the sessions.

Once you're married, ask your husband to do the same. He may resist a bit, because males don't always realize just how easily they can be manipulated and deceived by women. You may have to educate him to help him be aware that when a man has his stuff together, there will always be a woman or two around who just can't help herself. Only then will he be able to defend your marriage from all threats, seen and unseen.

Final Thoughts

Congratulations: You've made it to the end of a long and complicated book. Don't feel bad if some of it went over your head, because we have covered a tremendous amount of information and touched on some complex subjects. Just re-read the parts you feel fuzzy about, or the whole book if you prefer. At a minimum, re-read each chapter as you get to it in your dating process or relationship. If something still doesn't make sense or if you run in a situation I didn't cover, you can always contact me through my website for clarification (as well as sign up to see answers to other questions and hear about other success stories).

Always remember that Spirit doesn't need you to follow this system perfectly to bring you the marriage you were meant for. On the other hand, also remember that Spirit works on its timetable, not ours. If you are following the system and it's not working, check in with Spirit to see what the holdup might be. Spirit may need you to work on yourself a bit first or for you to be patient while other pieces fall into place. Always trust that Spirit loves you and that in Spirit's hands, all things work together for your highest good.

Blessings and best wishes on your quest.

P.S. I would love to hear your success stories and see pictures of you with your man. You can send them through my website. Just let me know if I can share your story and pictures.

APPENDIX I

The Selfish Gene

The concept that your genes want you to do things that are bad for you personally was first popularized in the 1976 book, The Selfish Gene by Richard Dawkins. Basically, Dawkins' theory states that genes that influence behavior often do so to increase the likelihood that the gene itself replicates by being passed on to the next generation in as many copies as possible as opposed to the survival of the individual. This is a twist on Charles Darwin's original theory of evolution of survival of the fittest organism to survival of the fittest genes or more accurately the survival of the genes that are the best at replicating themselves in generation after generation.

In other words, the genes that currently exist in the world today do so because they were the best at replicating themselves generation after generation throughout history, while organisms such as humans, plants and animals are merely a vehicle for the gene. This preference for the gene over the organism is so strong that in some species such as salmon and many types of flies, they die shortly after mating and passing on their genes to the next generation.

Even though humans live long after we are done reproducing (probably because it takes so long for a child to grow up and more than one person raising the child really helps), genes still have a powerful effect on our behavior. While we are able to think logically and have the ability to choose

193

our actions, genes exert their influence on our behavior most strongly through our emotions.

Lets use the example of the fear of public speaking to illustrate this point. Fear of public speaking is fairly common, but obviously there are people with no such fear. While you can learn to be afraid of public speaking (if you were criticized or shamed while speaking in front of a group), for most of us the fear of public speaking is innate, meaning we've always had it and there is no clear cause like a traumatic event. However, science knows from epidemiological research studies that the fear of public speaking tends to cluster in families. This familial association is so strong that the fear of public speaking still occurs in individuals even when adopted at birth by families with no such fear.

What this means is that most of the time the fear of public speaking is passed on through the genes and isn't learned or a product of one's environment. Similarly, our genes influence many of our emotions from fear and anger to even love and attraction. The genetic influence on sexual and romantic attraction is particularly strong. Have you ever wondered why you are attracted to men that look a certain way or have a certain personality type?

Science has been able to demonstrate that the most consistently attractive traits in males besides appearance (that are programed by our genes) are traits associated with "dominance", meaning traits that signify or are associated with being socially dominant. For example, fine clothes, jewelry and expensive cars signify that a man has access to resources and can support many children. Being physically strong and fit signifies than a man can fight to protect his mate and children as well as hunt large animals to feed them. High social standing such as being a member of a prominent family or the leader of an organized group such as a company or even a gang signify social dominance and thus priority access to resources and protection within the group. Even personality traits such as confidence and humor have been shown to correlate with high social status and its associated benefits.

However, the problem with relying on these markers of dominance is that a significant number of men have learned (or have genetic programing) to mimic being dominant. This is what bad boys do. They mimic having high social standing with displays of extreme confidence and disdain for rules. They mimic having access to resources by spending every dime they have (or can borrow or steal) on a fancy car, fancy clothes and bling. They mimic being able to fight and hunt by acting fearless and taking unnecessary risks.

The sad part is their act works on women even when women know that he doesn't have much social standing, doesn't have access to resources and being able to fight and hunt aren't particularly relevant anymore. Too many women fall for the chemistry such men can generate in them rather than men of quality that have social standing, solid careers and the ability to provide for a family. So don't settle for fool's gold. Hold out for the real thing, the solid gold of the quality man you were meant for.

How to Find a Psychotherapist

*T*hank you for taking the difficult step of being open to going to psychotherapy to improve your mental health, your relationships and your life. It takes a lot of courage and humility to let someone inside of our defenses and allow them to examine us at the deepest level. I know because I went to psychotherapy for 8 years earlier in my career as a psychiatrist. I did a particularly intrusive type of psychotherapy called psychoanalysis. It was hard and my therapist told me a lot of things about myself that I didn't want to hear and took a prolonged time for me to accept (hence the 8 years).

However, not everyone needs such a deep level of psychotherapy or spend such a long time in therapy. Depending on the issue or issues that need to be addressed, there are types of psychotherapy that are particularly adept at addressing certain types of issues and can work in as little as a few sessions. This is not an exhaustive list of all the various types of therapy (there are literally hundreds of types of psychotherapy), but I do address the three basic types of therapy that I recommend for various issues that come up. Obviously, if you have an issue I don't specifically address, you may need a different type of psychotherapy and will need to ask a mental health professional about what type of therapy to seek.

Cognitive-Behavioral Therapy (CBT)

Cognitive-behavioral therapy, which goes by the term CBT is the most commonly used and most scientifically researched type of psychotherapy. It has been scientifically proven to be effective for almost every type of depressive disorder (except Bipolar depression) and all of the various anxiety disorders. It is so widely used that almost every mental health professionals is trained in it (that doesn't mean every therapist actually choses to do CBT).

CBT works on the principle that our emotional states are actually caused by a thought or belief we have about an event or situation. For example, if you are in a car accident where your car is totaled (but you were not injured and you have good car insurance) how you feel about the car accident depends on what you thought about your car. If you thought your car was wonderful you would probably feel sad, but if you thought your car was a lemon you might feel excited about being able to get a different car with the check from the insurance company.

However, the second principle of CBT is that many of our negative feelings, from anxiety to depression, actually come from illogical and inaccurate thoughts and beliefs. It is these illogical/inaccurate thoughts and beliefs that CBT seeks to change by recognizing they are illogical and inaccurate and then replacing them with a logical and accurate thought or belief that results in a more positive emotion.

For example, if your best friend at work walks past you without acknowledging you, you might illogically think that your friend was angry with you despite a complete lack of evidence. More logically, you might recognize that you don't have enough information to make a judgment and merely wonder why your friend didn't acknowledge you. Later that day you might pull your friend aside and ask if they are okay. Your friend might then apologize for not seeing you and tell you about the meeting she had just walked out of where her boss criticized her job performance.

At first, it takes a lot of mental effort to monitor our thoughts to spot the illogical and inaccurate ones and then replace them, but over the next few weeks and months, the monitoring and replacing becomes so automatic that your subconscious takes over and you just have logical and accurate thoughts. Because this monitoring/replacing process is a mental skill, CBT often feels more like mental coaching than therapy. That is why I recommend reading a good book on CBT like Feeling Good by David Burns before you go to CBT because many people can learn the skills just from a book and make the therapy go faster, sometimes in as little as a handful of sessions.

Finding a psychotherapist that is adept at doing CBT is fairly easy since everyone is trained to do it and therapists that don't do it are upfront about it. Therapists that don't do CBT typically describe themselves as psychoanalysts or say they do psychodynamic, humanistic or existential psychotherapy, you just need to ask. Sometimes therapists will say they do "eclectic" psychotherapy, which means they do a little bit of everything. Just ask them if they are comfortable starting with CBT and not moving on to other types of therapy until you master CBT.

Don't be too focused on the therapist's level of training such as whether they have a PhD or just a master's degree because the most important factor in finding a therapist if that you feel comfortable with them and they seem to get you. If you have insurance, contact your insurance company to get the list of therapists that are on their panel of providers. Insurance company help lines also tend to know who on the panel is good and who is taking new clients. Otherwise ask your friends and even your doctor who is good in your area.

If you don't have insurance and you can't afford to pay cash, look for community mental health programs because they will often have sliding scales of fees based on your ability to pay and can cost as little as $20 per session. Also check with any local universities or hospitals because they may have mental health training programs and need clients for their students. Yes, you will be seeing a student, but a licensed mentor will closely supervise them and the cost is minimal or even free.

Psychodynamic Psychotherapy

CBT is tremendously useful for a vast range of emotional and even relationship problems, but it lacks the ability to work on our deepest relationship problems because such problems often caused by disruption to our attachment system (see Chapter Four – Bonding and Chemistry). While a variety of types of psychotherapy are able to repair attachment system damage, they generally fall under the broad title of psychodynamic psychotherapy (along with some forms of humanistic psychotherapy). As with CBT, almost every psychotherapist is trained to some degree in psychodynamic psychotherapy. So unless a therapist exclusively does CBT or some other specialized form of therapy its pretty safe to assume they do psychodynamic psychotherapy.

If you are not sure, just ask. They can tell you if what they specialize in is a type of psychodynamic therapy. A good example of this is the case of psychoanalysis, which is a type of psychodynamic psychotherapy and is possibly the purest form of psychodynamic psychotherapy. Therapists that do psychoanalysis are extremely well trained, but they often don't take insurance and can insist you commit to 2 or more years of therapy before they will agree to see you.

However, just as with CBT, it is not the level of training or the precise flavor of psychodynamic therapy a therapist does that is most important, but whether or not you feel comfortable with the therapist. Just be aware that psychodynamic therapy is a slow process and is often measured in terms of years rather than weeks or months when you are trying to heal your attachment system.

The other challenging thing about psychodynamic psychotherapy is that it unstructured and can feel like you are just talking about the same things over and over again with your therapist. Don't worry, that is how psychodynamic psychotherapy has to be done because it is non-linear and is more like a spiral where you loop around the same side over and over again, but at a slightly higher level on each pass. Just be patient with the process because it can take several loops before you can tell that even though you are covering the same ground again, you are doing so from a higher perspective. You also don't tend to feel much different as the therapy progresses. You will know it's working when you find yourself in a situation that would have triggered you in the past, but you handle it well without much drama or distress.

As with finding a therapist that does CBT, start with your insurance company help line to find a psychodynamic psychotherapist on their panel. You insurance also can tell you what kind of therapy they do, whether members tend to like them and if they are taking new clients. If you don't have insurance, check with your local community mental health programs to see if they use a sliding scale for their fees based on your ability to pay. Otherwise, check with any local universities and hospitals for psychotherapy training programs that offer low cost or even free therapy.

Dialectical Behavioral Therapy (DBT)

DBT is a highly specialized form of therapy that was designed to treat self-destructive behavior such as recurrent suicide attempts and cutting that other forms of therapy struggle to treat. Such self-destructive behavior is often found in people with severe attachment system damage (such as a disorganized attachment style) and tends to interfere with psychodynamic psychotherapy.

DBT was originally designed as an intensive two-year outpatient treatment program that was run by a team of therapists. However, more recent research indicates that weekly therapy with a therapist using DBT techniques can be effective as well, which is great because formal DBT programs can be hard to find and may not be covered by insurance.

The other challenge of DBT is that it only works on the self-destructive behavior and you still need to do psychodynamic psychotherapy after the DBT to heal the attachment disruptions. If you find a therapist that does both DBT style individual therapy and psychodynamic psychotherapy (and most do) you can start with DBT and smoothly move in to psychodynamic psychotherapy when you are ready without having to find a new therapist.

Again, contact your insurance company to help you find a DBT therapist (as opposed to a DBT program) that is on their panel. When you contact the DBT therapists on the panel, just be sure to ask if they will continue to see you for psychodynamic psychotherapy after the DBT is over. If you don't have insurance, check with any local community mental health programs to see if they have a sliding scale of fees based on income. I would be hesitant to go to a university or hospital based training program and see a student unless there was no other option for therapy because DBT is an advanced form of psychotherapy that requires a solid foundation in the other forms of therapy to do effectively.

When you find a DBT therapist, go with them, because there still aren't that many DBT therapists and feeling comfortable with your therapist is not as important in DBT as with the other types of therapy. It is not usual for people to dislike their DBT therapist at first and them love them by the end of DBT when its time to start psychodynamic psychotherapy.

Substance Abuse (Addiction) Therapy

I want to briefly address the question of substance abuse treatment. Most psychotherapists are comfortable working with someone with a mild substance use disorder such as with marijuana or ecstasy use and minor alcohol problems. However, more severe substance use such as hard drugs (pain pills, heroin, cocaine, LSD, Ketamine, speed, methamphetamine, etc.) or severe alcohol use that causes withdrawal requires treatment by someone who specializes in treating substance use disorders.

Substance use specialists typically work in substance use treatment centers and programs because treatment often requires a combination of specialties including medical doctors to manage the physical withdrawal, psychiatrists to treat associated mental health disorders and counselors to run therapy groups and teach recovery skills. Most cities have treatment programs, many of which are publically funded so you can be treated even if you don't have insurance. The challenge is often the length of the waiting list for publicly funding program, but keep checking back because many people on the waiting list don't show up and you may be able to take their place.

Finally, don't forget about Alcoholics Anonymous (AA) and Narcotics Anonymous (NA). Even though professional treatment is superior, they are still effective and have helped millions of people get and stay sober over the years. They are also free and can provide long-term support to help you maintain your sobriety. You can also get a sponsor who can be available to you day or night. Just don't date anyone you meet at AA/NA because you are better off being with someone who has never had a substance use problem (as long as he is willing to support your sobriety by not using himself).

20815796R00135

Printed in Great Britain
by Amazon